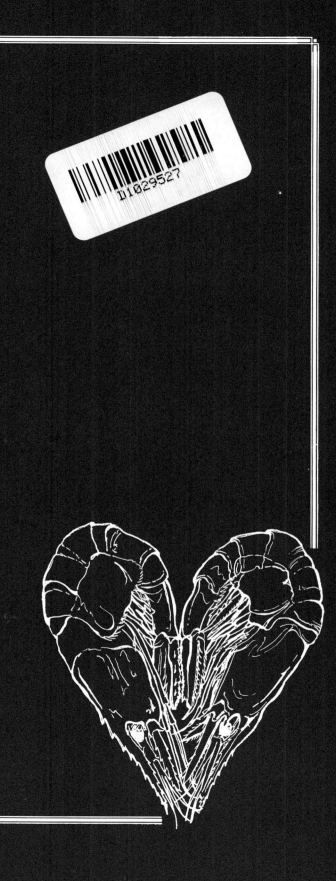

The Food of Love

THE
FOOD OF LOVE

Judith Hann

Partridge Press

Home Economists
Lucy Knox
Elaine Andrews

Loan of tableware
The Reject Shop, Windsor

Photography and Styling
Sue Atkinson, Mike Roles Studio

Design and illustration by
Victor Shreeve

Published in Great Britain by
Partridge Press, Maxwelton House, Boltro Road, Haywards Heath, West Sussex

(Partridge Press is an imprint of Transworld Publishers Limited,
61/63 Uxbridge Road, London W5 5JA)

Typeset by August Filmsetting, Haydock, St. Helens

Printed and bound in Great Britan by
W.S. Cowell Limited, Ipswich

ISBN 1-85225-025-9

CONTENTS

INTRODUCTION

This book is for everyone who loves food, and who regards cooking as the perfect way of showing their love for their partner, family and friends. The recipes are healthy and seasonal, and use ingredients which never thicken the waistlines and arteries of those you most care for. But none of the dishes are brown and boring, like so much 'health' food. This is definitely not a book for faddies. It is for foodies, for intelligent cooks who realize that healthy eating should never be a penance, and that the latest scientific thinking on reducing fats and salt, while increasing fibre and vitamin-rich foods, is totally compatible with much of the finest traditional cuisine.

I firmly believe that food should be beautifully and elegantly presented whenever possible, and my *Food of Love*, like love itself, is very special, creative, lavish, and often surprising. My recipes make use of the fresh and best of British produce: our fish, vegetables, game and fruit. The British style of cooking has been out of favour for some time, but it is now as easy to eat well in this country as it is in France and other parts of the world. We should be proud of our excellent, local produce. We should be fascinated by the recipes handed down from earlier generations. I collect old cookery books, and sift the healthy eating ideas from the many unhealthy ones. Some of these 'old' ideas reappear in my recipes. Game with fruit sauces, spiced quince and other preserves: these have been enjoyed in Britain for centuries.

But I also cook food which originates from other countries. I have found that many of the great dishes of the world can be modified to become healthy. There may be no substitute for love, but there are now plenty of substitutes for the unhealthy ingredients – the cream, butter and fatty meats – of famous recipes. I have banned those ingredients from my kitchen, without reducing the flavour of my food, so that *The Food of Love* not only looks and tastes good, it is good for your health too.

It will keep you slim, without the need to resort to a special diet. It will protect you from the diseases of affluence, like diabetes, cancer, strokes and heart disease, which can be caused by eating too much fat, too much sugar, too much salt, or too much animal protein. By using my recipes, you will increase your intake of fresh fruit and vegetables; you will eat more healthy, unrefined carbohydrates; you will increase the fibre in your diet, while the healthier cooking techniques will ensure that you are having enough essential minerals and vitamins.

The change to healthier eating habits has been shown to have a dramatic effect. In America for example, it helped to reduce heart disease by 20 per cent in the 1970s. Improvements are just beginning to be seen in Britain, too. 'Health food' sales are rising; but gourmets who want to be healthy have been neglected, and many people are still unsure how to eat healthily *and* lavishly.

So *The Food of Love* explains the cooking techniques which retain the goodness of good food. It shows how to get the most out of herbs and spices to compensate for reducing salt. It offers ideas for low-fat yoghurt, *fromage blanc*, and margarine and oils high in polyunsaturates, to use instead of unhealthy cream and butter. And it features recipes for fish, offal, poultry and game, which are all better for us than red meats, like fatty beef and lamb.

My style of cooking is newer than *Nouvelle Cuisine* and healthier than *Cuisine Minceur*, although they both taught me a great deal. *Nouvelle Cuisine* was refreshing and glamorous when it first arrived in our restaurants and homes, but it still uses 'heart attack ingredients', like butter and cream. It just serves them prettily in small portions on vast plates.

Cuisine Minceur was written by Michel Guérard with slimming in mind. Like many successful chefs, he was becoming overweight, so his wife, Christine, encouraged him to use different ingredients, like sugar substitutes and lots of vegetables. This book changed my thinking, introducing the idea of using low-fat substances, like *fromage blanc*, instead of cream. I gave the book to my husband, complete with packets of seeds to grow the herbs which feature in the book, like sorrel and chervil. It was presented to him on Valentine's Day, inscribed with the words: 'The Food of Love'. Without me realizing it, until several years later, the idea for *this* book had been born.

But my recipes are far simpler than Guérard's, and use 'natural' rather than slimming ingredients, like wholemeal flour and brown rice, and muscovado sugar instead of substitutes. My food, if you like, is healthy *haute cuisine*. I prefer to go shopping without too many fixed ideas, so that the evening meal is inspired by the very best seasonal ingredients on offer. Boredom with ingredients leads to poor cooking.

On a recent trip to Lyons, I went to the markets early in the morning with Pierre Bourrilot, one of the city's great chefs. He told me he didn't prepare his menus until he knew what the local market gardeners and farmers had to offer on the day. The range was exciting.

But excellent food does not depend on a long list of elaborate ingredients. It is quite the reverse. If I see a recipe with more than 10 ingredients, I worry, because I have found that 'maximum ingredients usually means minimum of flavour.' In the same way, I loathe elaborate, foreign names for recipes, and menus full of prose like: '. . . served with sun-kissed grapes.' My recipes have British names, which rarely sound that exciting. But they are British recipes, using mainly British ingredients. And if they taste good and are healthy, that is good enough for me. I have always felt that while French restaurants have a right to use glamorous Gallic phrases on their menus, the rest of us have not.

We have plenty of fascinating British names ourselves, particularly for the wide range of vegetables and fruit grown here. There are said to be over five million serious gardeners in Britain, and I am now one of the growing band. Seed catalogues are amazing, with an ever-increasing range of vegetables with lovely names on offer, that are more often grown today for taste than appearance. Fruit and vegetable shops are getting more adventurous, too. Pink Fir potatoes, for example, have just made a welcome return. Even supermarkets stock this tasty tuber, which looks rather like a Jerusalem artichoke. There is also more choice of organically grown produce in local shops.

Fewer people are happy to live on frozen produce, which does not change from season to season, and supermarket tomatoes and apples, which are chosen for their predictable size and colour rather than their taste. Living from the freezer makes the taste buds atrophy, and takes us back to that primitive and ugly situation where people 'eat to live'. I am not suggesting that we should 'live to eat', but as we *have* to eat, we might as well enjoy it and put a lot of effort into our cooking.

I decided that on the first day that 'I was on my own' after leaving home and university. I had never cooked; I did not even know how to scramble an egg when my new husband first ordered his breakfast; but as I would be cooking most days for the rest of my life, it seemed sensible and more enjoyable to try and do it well. I have never resented the time spent on food. At first I pored over basic books, and made annoying mistakes in the kitchen. I moved on to Elizabeth David, Claudia Roden, Julia Child, Jane Grigson and many other in-

spiring cookery writers, and then later I only read books for inspiration. The recipes were my own.

I began to agree with the American author who wrote: 'Cooking is a sport without a season'. It is never boring. It is an exciting, artistic business, where others share your pleasure. Cooking demands inspiration, hard work, humour, and above all love. And the proportions of these ingredients will vary from time to time. I pity people who regard cooking as a waste of time and money. Why can't they see that it is a satisfying way of giving love to others, and of encouraging your family and friends to spend precious time relaxing and talking together? I think that cooking is a more satisfactory art than painting a picture. The end product may have disappeared by the next day, but the memory of good food, enjoyed during a stimulating few hours spent around the dining table, can never be taken away.

My last word on this subject comes from a scientist; a biochemist called Anthony Harris, from the North London Polytechnic. He believes that if you do not enjoy eating with your partner, then there is something very wrong with your relationship and your sex life: 'Preparing food and eating it together has always been an expression of intimacy between couples, so it follows that when that stops, the intimacy has been broken.' Eating together provides time to be relaxed and outspoken, giving the opportunity to say things which perhaps cannot be said elsewhere.

And I believe that what applies to couples, applies also to family and friends. The experts have also said that if your children are still talking in depth with you when they are 16, they are going to be close to you for life. Time spent over dinner provides that regular time to talk to your family and friends. *The Food of Love* is not only about beautiful, healthy and well-presented food. It is also about showing your love, and giving your time and talent, to the people who matter most.

RECIPE INGREDIENTS EXPLAINED

All recipes are based on servings for four people.

Oven temperatures are referred to as
Low (325°F/160°C/Gas No. 3)   Medium (375°F/190°C/Gas No. 5)
Hot (450°F/230°C/Gas No. 8)

BREADCRUMBS	Made freshly from wholemeal bread.
FLOUR	Always wholemeal.
HERBS	These should be fresh whenever possible. They are now sold by most supermarkets. If you have to use dried herbs, halve the quantity.
MARGARINE	Always use high in polyunsaturates. Some are salt-free. These should be used sparingly in cooking, and never when food has to be cooked in very hot fat. Many margarines break up when the heat is raised. So, although margarine can be used for gently softening vegetables, when food has to be browned, use oil.
MILK	Skimmed or semi-skimmed.
OIL	Oils high in polyunsaturates, like sunflower oil.
OLIVE OIL	When this is listed, it is used because the taste of the oil is important to the recipe. A good-quality olive oil, like extra-virgin, can make all the difference. Use green-coloured oil, not yellow.
PARMESAN	Always use freshly grated cheese. A small block of Parmesan keeps well in the fridge.
PEPPER	This means freshly ground black pepper, unless stated otherwise.
RICE	Brown rice, unless otherwise stated.
SALT	Salt is rarely used in my recipes, and taste-buds soon adjust. Most food tastes better without salt, but there are exceptions. Artichokes and corn, for example, do need salt to bring out the flavour. Salt substitutes are quite successful, and have been accepted by my family.
STOCK	This should preferably be home-made. If stock cubes are used, be careful with the final taste of the soup or sauce, because they are salty.
SUGAR	Muscovado.

HEALTHY COOKING METHODS

Several years ago, the first thing I did when I decided to cook only healthy food, was to abandon the 'chip pan' I had used for deep-frying. If it was there, I decided I might be tempted to use it occasionally, because deep-frying is easy, quick and makes food look crisp, brown and appealing.

In the same way, I banned cream and butter from the kitchen. If they were in the fridge, I would give in to temptation, because both make food taste and look good.

But I did not miss any of these temptations for long. Grilled food, in fact, tastes better. There are perfectly adequate, and healthy, replacements for butter and cream. And there are also many cooking techniques which produce moist, tasty food without the need to use fat, sugar and salt.

STEAMING is a perfect cooking technique for vegetables, fish and grains. It retains more of the food's taste, nutrients and colour. For steaming, the simplest piece of equipment to buy, which fits inside a normal saucepan, is made of overlapping steel plates in the form of a basket on short legs. I also have a very useful tall steamer which takes three separate steaming trays, so that different foods can be cooked simultaneously. The wok is also used for steaming, by using the grid, and covering it with its domed lid. Chinese bamboo steamers are particularly attractive: several small round baskets with slatted bases can be fitted together over boiling water to produce a wide range of subtle vegetables and steamed Chinese dishes. It is also possible to buy electric steamers, which simplify the whole business for serious cooks. Remember to retain the juices produced when steaming to add to sauces and soups.

GRILLING is so much healthier than frying, because it reduces the amount of fat in meat. It is best for tender cuts of meat and for the healthy oily fish, like sardine, mackerel and herring. Take care with delicate white fish and chicken or pork fillet. They do dry out quickly and should, therefore, only be grilled for a very short time.

BARBECUEING should follow similar rules. Just like grilling, it is healthy because it forces out the fat, while preserving flavour. Hard, lump-wood charcoal is better than briquettes, because it reaches an ideal temperature more quickly. The right time to start cooking is when a thin layer of white ash has formed. Add herbs, fir-cones and fruit-wood to improve the smell and flavour.

REDUCING a sauce by evaporation produces a healthier and better-tasting end result than thickening with flour, cream or egg yolks. A shallow pan gives the fastest results. Just bubble the sauce vigorously and watch constantly. Check for seasoning after the sauce has reached an ideal consistency.

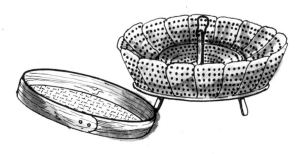

WOK COOKING is so satisfying that I now have three woks in regular use. Food is quickly fried, using very little oil, so that colour, flavour and nutrients are preserved. You get the best results with evenly sized pieces of meat, fish or vegetables. Then they cook in the same amount of time. Remember to stir or turn the food constantly.

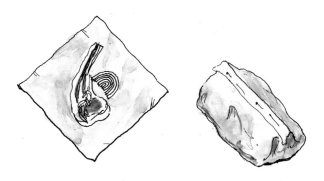

COOKING IN PARCELS OF FOIL OR GREASEPROOF PAPER in the oven is another way of preserving flavour and goodness. I use it a lot for fish, but it is also good for meat, vegetables and fruit. Serve favourite mixed fresh fruits, flavoured with a vanilla pod, in a foil parcel. Cook in a hot oven for several minutes, and let people unwrap them at the table. It makes an aromatic and surprising dessert.

FOOD PROCESSING is useful for many recipes, particularly for making soups and sauces quickly and simply. Food processors have blades which chop and liquidize, and equipment for grating, shredding, slicing, making dough and so on. When I say 'process' or 'purée' in my recipes, you can liquidize the food in a blender, or use a normal sieve, or Mouli rotating sieve, if you don't have a food processor.

MARINATING food adds flavour and reduces the need for lengthy cooking. The food is normally immersed for hours or even days in an acid liquid, flavoured with spices and herbs. The acid makes the food more tender by breaking down its fibres. Fish is often marinated before eating raw.

BLANCHING food in boiling water from a few seconds to a couple of minutes, then putting it in cold water, softens it a little, and intensifies the colour, making the tougher vegetables suitable for adding to salads.

EATING RAW FOODS is the simplest way to guarantee healthy food. Nutrients and colour are preserved. We should all be eating a high percentage of raw foods, but salads can be dull. Innovation and presentation are both important here.

TERRACOTTA COOKING BRICKS for meat, chicken, fish and potatoes produce tender, succulent food. This brick method imitates the primitive clay ovens, which cook food very slowly in an enclosed environment. You do need a different cooking brick for each different type of food, because the terracotta absorbs flavours. You do not need to add any fat. Try a potato cooker for the first tubers of the season. It is the perfect method for retaining flavour. With chicken or fish, I just pop in fresh herbs, and perhaps half a lemon into the animal's cavity, add a little pepper, and cook very slowly. The juices are then used to make a subtle sauce. I have also got a terracotta tandoori oven, which produces succulent kebabs and whole chickens, cooked over an enclosed barbecue, inside a sort of terracotta chimney. I can recommend it.

HEALTHY OILS

New oils appear on the market with confusing regularity, attempting to appeal with their low cost, their 'true' taste, or their health claims. The truth is that most of them should be totally ignored. They go through so much processing that they end up tasteless, useless and possibly unhealthy, too. Avoid all blended vegetable or cooking oils, because you cannot be sure exactly what they contain.

All a kitchen really needs is a good olive oil, a general-purpose oil, which is high in polyunsaturated fats, and then a selection of luxury oils for flavouring, like sesame, walnut and hazelnut oils.

A cooking oil is healthy only if it contains the right kind of fatty acids. Saturated fatty acids are the ones to avoid, and they are found in high quantities in both coconut and palm oils. Polyunsaturated fatty acids are much healthier. Some research suggests they help to prevent blood clots forming. Oils which are high in polyunsaturates and low in saturated fat are safflower, sunflower, soya, corn and walnut. Those low in saturated fat include olive, sesame, almond and hazelnut.

Olive oil was the first, and is still the best, of all cooking oils. I use is when taste is important – for example, in salad-dressings – although for general cooking I use sunflower oil, because it contains the healthy polyunsaturates. Like wine, olive oil varies, depending on where, when and how it was grown and made. And again like wine, it can be very expensive, especially the cold-pressed, extra-virgin olive oil. Of all the healthy oils, safflower is highest in polyunsaturated fats at 75 per cent; sunflower has a good texture; corn is too heavy in texture for salads; and soya is cheap but can smell fishy.

Of all the oils which add a lot of flavour, my favourites are sesame and walnut. I use both in many recipes.

Sesame oil can be subtle, particularly the French ones, or very strongly seedy and toasted, as in many of the Chinese ranges. I use this oil, combined with root ginger and sometimes soy sauce, with chicken, fish and prawn dishes. When I take the top off the bottle, saliva always flows: the smell is just perfect.

Walnut oil, like the other oils made from nuts, can be used for cooking, but is ruined if the heat is turned too high. Oils made from nuts are extremely expensive, but their flavour is also very special. If they are stored in a cool, dark place, they will last a long time. They are produced by being crushed and then heated to give the oils their toasted flavour.

The nut oils make excellent salad-dressings, combined with a good wine vinegar, or in the case of walnut oil, with cider vinegar. I usually add the relevant toasted nuts to the dressings, like walnuts to the quail salad on page 114, and for heating through the Jerusalem artichokes and shallots on page 38.

When using almonds in stir-fried dishes, cook with a little almond oil. This oil is also useful in puddings, and goes particularly well with peaches and apricots.

HEALTHY CREAMY COOKING

It is now possible to make traditional recipes, which normally use cream, with healthier, substitute ingredients. And in most cases, these substitutes are low-fat, soft cheeses. They sound grim, which the lumpy cottage cheeses certainly are, but there are many others, which are useful and tasty.

Unfortunately, there are so many cream substitutes on sale now that confusion has set in. If you go to any large, on-the-ball supermarket these days, you are likely to be confronted with dozens of different plastic containers in the dairy department. Alongside the double cream and fruit yoghurts, there will be Jockey, *crème fraîche*, *fromage blanc*, Quark, Greek yoghurt, ewe's milk yoghurt, ricotta, *crème fleurette*, and many more.

So what does it all mean? Well, for a start, *fromage blanc* is the same thing as *fromage frais*. There are different makes, which vary in fat content. Reading labels is particularly important with these foods. Jockey is a popular make, but the fat content of this *fromage frais* is higher than some others. *Crème fraîche* contains 30 per cent fat, which sounds high, but is in fact only half as fatty as clotted cream. It is excellent with fruit, but I feel it contains too much fat for regular use. The thick Greek yoghurt tastes wonderful, but at 10 per cent fat, it is less healthy than many natural yoghurts. You can make your own thick yoghurt, as I describe on page 19, containing much less fat. Cottage cheese contains about 4 per cent fat, but I don't like it for cooking.

FROMAGE BLANC

This low-fat, creamy substance has been popular in France for some time, and is now appearing in most of our supermarkets. It has a bland taste, which is less acid than yoghurt, and can be used as a substitute for cream in many recipes, even being served instead of cream with desserts. Watch out for the label on the tubes, because the amount of fat varies enormously from 8 per cent to 0.4 per cent. The lower-fat varieties taste excellent.

QUARK

This resembles *fromage blanc*, but it has a more acid taste, and I therefore find it more useful for savoury recipes. It is also more solid in texture, and needs care to blend into sauces. Again look for the lower–fat varieties which are sold in supermarkets now, and even local corner shops. Silhouette Quark varies from 0 to 4.5 and 10 per cent fat.

RICOTTA

Italian shops and delicatessens sell this useful low-fat, unsalted cheese. Made from goat's, cow's or ewe's milk, it is delicious fresh or cooked. I use it in lasagne, to stuff cannelloni and pancakes, and mixed with milk as a base for creamy sauces to serve with noodles. Ricotta contains only 4 per cent fat.

FOOD BASICS

I now find it very easy to track down healthy ingredients. Brown rice and pasta, healthy oils, good fish and low-fat meats are available at all large supermarkets these days. But I also find it useful to make a few of my own basic foods for healthy recipies, like low-fat yoghurts and cheese, and sprouted seeds which are full of vitamins for fresh salads.

Bread is something I rarely make, partly because I prefer to give any spare time to other types of cooking, but also because I am lucky enough to have an excellent baker nearby. Anyone with the time, however, can get a lot of pleasure from making bread. The health rules are the same whether you make your own or buy bread: always make sure it is stone-ground, 100 per cent whole-wheat or wholemeal flour or bread. It is certainly not enough to ask for 'brown bread'. Many so-called 'healthy' brown loaves are definitely not good for you. They can be full of additives, and the brown colour can come just from caramel. So it is worth checking carefully before you buy. Healthy bread is extremely good for you; far better than raw bran sprinkled on cereals, and as time goes on it becomes easier to find the right, stone-ground loaves.

SPROUTING SEEDS is something that I enjoy doing, and it is extremely worthwhile, providing cheap fresh salad ingredients, as well as bean sprouts for Chinese stir-frying. There are many different types of seeds worth sprouting, from the more normal mung beans, to whole lentils, chick-peas, aduki beans, alfalfa and mustard cress. The smaller seeds look particularly attractive once they have been sprouted, washed and added to salads, but all of them are useful and healthy, being full of important vitamins and minerals.

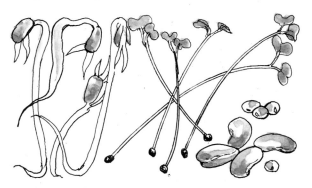

You can sprout seeds in any large glass jar. First soak them overnight, then drain and put in the jar. Put in a warm place with the opening covered. Rinse and drain the seeds well every day, and after about three days put in the sunlight. Within about another three days they will be tasty to eat. So tip them into water, remove any husks and put in the fridge until you wish to use them. Some shops now sell three-tier plastic salad sprouters which makes rinsing and draining much easier, because there are small holes at the base of each of the three plastic dishes. It also means, of course, that you can grow three types of seeds at the same time.

PASTRY is another useful basic to have standing-by in the fridge. I don't use a great deal in my cooking, and I stopped using white and puffed pastry long ago; but there are times when I like to use the Greek filo pastry which is stocked by many supermarkets, and I make my own whole-wheat pastry for both sweet and savoury dishes.

Whole-wheat pastry

8 oz/225 g whole-wheat flour
1 tsp baking powder
2 oz/50 g oil
2 oz/50 g margarine
about 2 tbsp water (or a little more to mix)

Sift the flour and baking powder together in a mixing bowl. Rub the margarine into the flour, then add the oil and water, and mix to a soft dough. Leave for about 15 minutes in a cool place before rolling out. This is enough for a 10 inch/25 cm flan case.

Fromage blanc pastry

This is perfect for spinach tart, small turnovers or for creamy-tasting flans, like my courgette flan on page 76. It is easiest to make using a food processor.

4 oz/100 g whole-wheat flour
4 oz/100 g margarine
4 oz/100 g thick *fromage blanc* or Silhouette Quark

Mix well. Then put the sticky dough in the fridge for an hour or two. If using for a flan, bake for about 20 minutes in a hot oven.

YOGHURT

Making yoghurt at home is both satisfying and money-saving. A large wide-necked vacuum flask is useful for this, although I was recently given a special yoghurt-maker as a present, which makes the job even easier because it has a thermometer. I find that thick Greek-style yoghurts are the most useful. They are solid enough to thicken savoury sauces and casseroles well, and with whipped egg-whites added, they make the best kind of substitute for thick cream to go with fruit puddings. It is now easy to find these Greek yoghurts in the shops, but watch the label because some are rather too high in fats. Pearl of Cyprus have now brought out a yoghurt of this type with less than 2 per cent fat, compared to the normal 10 per cent. I use this low-fat yoghurt as the basis of my home-made version.

Home-made yoghurt

1 pt/600 ml skimmed milk (this makes a thicker yoghurt than whole milk)
2 tbsp natural yoghurt
2 tbsp skimmed-milk powder

Scald the milk and leave to cool slightly. If you use a thermometer, cool the milk to about 45°C – or until you can put a finger in it comfortably. Then stir in the yoghurt and the skimmed-milk powder. Do not use the powder unless you want a thick yoghurt. I often make two batches, one thick for sauces and one of a thinner consistency for eating normally. Put into flask or any container you like to use. Leave overnight in a warm place, when it should be set. Refrigerate in a clean container, when it should thicken even more.

You can also produce an even thicker yoghurt, which you can use like curd cheese, by putting the yoghurt in a muslin cloth and leaving to drain for a few hours.

CHEESE

Curd cheese is normally made from milk rather than yoghurt. It is easy to do at home, and once made will keep in the fridge for one week at least. It has a much fresher taste than the commercial varieties, and you can be sure that it contains no additives when you make it yourself.

Home-made curd cheese

1 pt/600 ml whole milk
¼ pt/150 ml buttermilk
1 tbsp lemon juice

Scald the milk in a pan and leave to cool to about 20°C. Stir in the buttermilk and heat to about 75°C. Leave to cool, stirring every few minutes, and adding the lemon juice to help the curds form. When the curds have separated from the whey, drain off the whey, using muslin, until the curds are firm.

From this basic curd cheese, I make several savoury cheeses.

SAUCES

I find it very useful to keep ready-made healthy sauces in the freezer or the fridge. During late September I buy pounds of cheap tomatoes when growers are clearing out their glasshouses. Tomatoes are often at their best flavour at this time, and because they are a funny shape – too small or squashed – they sell for a fraction of their normal price. The good, small ones are stored whole in the freezer for adding to dishes throughout the winter and spring. I make gallons of this basic tomato sauce.

Tomato sauce

For every 1 lb/450 g tomatoes, use:

1 tbsp oil
1 onion
1 large clove garlic
2 tbsp tomato purée
half cup of good strong stock
pepper
1 tbsp basil

Heat the oil and soften the onion, and then for a shorter time the garlic. Add the skinned and chopped tomatoes, and all the other ingredients. Simmer for 30 minutes. Purée and check the seasoning. Tabasco can be added to this just before serving, if a hotter sauce is needed. If basil is not available, marjoram, bay or thyme can be used instead.

White sauce

This forms the basis of many sauces, especially cheese sauces, made mild by adding *fromage blanc*, which is excellent for pasta dishes like lasagna, or made into a sauce with a stronger flavouring using a low-fat, hard cheese. By using whole-wheat flour, the sauce has a more interesting flavour.

For every pint of skimmed milk, you need:

3 tbsp oil
2 oz/50 g whole-wheat flour
pepper to taste
1 small onion
1 bay-leaf
pinch of mace
some peppercorns

Heat the milk. Then add the onion, bay-leaf, mace and peppercorns. Leave to stand for about 15 minutes. Strain the milk off. Heat the oil. Gently add the flour when the oil is still only warm, and stir well for a few minutes. Then add the milk gradually, stirring until smooth. Simmer for about 5 minutes and check seasoning.

Cocktail sauce

When you want to use a cocktail sauce with seafood, it is possible to make an interesting variety using yoghurt instead of mayonnaise.

6 oz/175 g plain yoghurt
$\frac{1}{2}$ tsp ground cumin
$\frac{1}{2}$ tsp paprika
black pepper to taste
1 tbsp lemon juice
1 tbsp tomato purée

FRUIT SAUCES

In the summer, when red berries, like raspberries, strawberries and red currants, are around, I make a summer fruit coulis to use with whole fruits, fruit sorbets and my favourite fruit and yoghurt ice-creams. The basic recipe is on page 91.

PASTA

If you are lucky, your doctor will be interested enough in preventative medicine to give you good advice on what to eat and how to exercise in order to have more chance of avoiding heart disease, obesity, cancer and many other diseases of Western Civilization. Many doctors have started telling their patients to 'eat like an Italian'. Southern Europeans have fewer heart attacks than the British, because they use olive oil instead of our dairy fats; cook more fish and poultry than beef and pork; and eat far more fresh fruit and vegetables than we do.

Many British people holidaying in Italy taste all the pasta and pizza, and see a lot of fat Italians, and come back home thinking they have sampled an unhealthy cuisine. But, in fact, pasta is extremely good for you, unless it is served with a rich, fatty sauce. Look for light and simple sauces in Italian recipe books. There are plenty of them to choose from.

There is also a wide choice of over 100 varieties of pasta, with wonderful names like farfalle, gnocchi, rigatoni, penne and tagliatelle. The small pasta shapes are best for soups and salads. The thin shapes, like tagliatelle and spaghetti, are used with hot sauces. The large tubes and sheets, including cannelloni, lasagne and penne, are stuffed or cooked in layers. I am particularly fond of whole-wheat pasta.

With all pasta, do make sure that you don't cook it for too long. It must always have a bite to it. I use a lot of fresh pasta, which often only needs two or three minutes cooking. I regularly record commentaries at a studio in central London, on the fringes of Soho, and whenever I go there, return home with fresh pasta and cheese from a wonderful Italian delicatessan.

Home-made pasta

I also make my own pasta, although I am no expert. Colouring it is even more difficult, particularly with squid ink. What should be glamorous black can easily turn out shabby grey. But green pasta, flavoured with spinach, or orange pasta, flavoured with tomato, are a bit easier. An Italian shop I use in London suggests making pasta from:

10 oz/275 g strong white flour
3 oz/75 g of semolina flour
half an egg
water as required

But you can make pasta without the special semolina flour in the following way:

10 oz/275 g strong white flour
1 large egg
1 tbsp olive oil
water as required

Beat the egg with the oil, and add the flour with some of the water. Add more water gradually, until the dough is soft. Knead it for about 15 minutes, then leave covered for about an hour. It is ready for rolling out after this time.

Whole-wheat pasta

Can be made from:

8 oz/225 g whole-wheat flour
4 oz/100 g plain flour
4 eggs

There are so many sauces I cannot include them here. But look in Italian books for meat-less sauces. Herbs, nuts and vegetables are excellent with pasta. When recipes demand cream, substitute low-fat ricotta cheese, mixed with milk.

HEALTHY VEGETABLES

If I had to be stranded on a desert island with only one type of food, I would choose vegetables. I get so excited by my first vegetables of the season that I often eat just a plateful of plain vegetables, flavoured perhaps with pepper and lemon juice, instead of salt and butter. Vegetables, cooked well, are fresh, invigorating and healthy.

I do not know how people managed before the eighteenth century, when the term vegetable was used for the first time. Only then did people begin to eat 'herbs and roots grown for food'. But even by Victorian times, the variety was still extremely limited, and until recently the British tended to eat meat with 'two veg' – veg that were often cooked so long that they were tasteless.

Now we can buy and grow a wide variety. In fact, greengrocers' displays have changed far more than butchers' and fishmongers' offerings. People are buying more vegetables; they are choosing them younger; and they are cooking them better. They realize that vegetables add colour, texture and healthy fibre, vitamins and minerals to their food. Here are some of my vegetable rules:

● Grow your own, or buy vegetables which are in season, and preferably local. Buy regularly in small quantities to ensure freshness. When we use our home-grown produce, we pick just before eating.
● Leave the skins on, only peeling vegetables when really necessary.
● Never soak vegetables in water, because the nutrients can leach out. Wash quickly.
● Cook in the shortest possible time, and do not start vegetables off in cold water: it lengthens the cooking time.
● Keep green vegetables out of the sun, because vitamins can be lost in sunlight.
● B vitamins are soluble in water, so it is worth keeping cooking water for soups.
● Use lemon juice, and never bicarbonate of soda, to retain the colour of vegetables. Bicarb destroys vitamins.
● Salt in cooking water encourages the loss of iron.
● Sugar in cooking water keeps cauliflowers white, and emphasizes the natural sweetness of root vegetables, like carrots, turnips and onions.
● Steam vegetables, or cook in very little water with a lid on the pan.
● Use stainless steel, enamel or glass pans for cooking. Aluminium oxidizes food.

SALADS

There are now dozens of different salad ingredients available, which add surprising tastes and eye-appeal to recipes. All should be bought as near as possible to the time they will be eaten, or if you grow your own, picked and washed just before a meal. When we had our first allotment I was warned to be ready to make beetroot and mustard salad one evening. But my husband brought home our first lettuce, which was so perfect it demanded to be eaten straightaway – so I made Caesar salad instead.

When it is necessary to store salads, two kinds of lettuce which keep well are Iceberg and Little Gem. Chinese leaves and the red lettuce, radicchio, are best separated into leaves, washed, dried and stored wrapped up in a tea-towel inside a plastic bag in the fridge. Chicory and endive only keep a very short time. Corn salad bruises easily, so it should always be kept in a rigid container. Store watercress immersed in cold water up to the base of the leaves.

Here are some of my favourite ingredients for salads:

BATAVIA is a type of endive with a bitter taste, which looks like curly lettuce.

CHICORY is the small, cream-coloured, spear-shaped vegetable with tightly-packed white leaves. It is pleasantly bitter when raw and combines well with all citrus fruits. Blanching reduces the bitterness.

CHINESE LEAVES are useful because the delicate inner leaves can be used raw in salads, and the layer of outer leaves should be cooked. They are a very convenient size and shape for stuffing with rice and meat mixtures.

CORN SALAD is also called lamb's lettuce or mache. The tangy, dark-green leaves are an interesting, pretty addition to salads.

ENDIVE is crisp, bitter and frizzy.

KALE can be shredded for winter salads.

RADICCHIO is often called 'designer lettuce' because it is such an attractive, dark-red colour, and because it became a bit of a cliché in trendy restaurants in the early Eighties. Again it has a bitter flavour, and looks lovely in mixed salads.

SORREL is not always easy to buy, but it is extremely easy to grow. My small crop self-seeds year after year. It is perfect for fish sauces and interesting soups, but also adds a sharp buzz to the best salads.

DANDELION LEAVES are refreshing and peppery eaten raw when they are young, but the older leaves are so bitter that they should be blanched. They classic way of eating them in France is with crisp bacon. I'm lucky enough to have eaten this for the first time at L'Hermitage hotel in Monte Carlo, and was so impressed that I rushed out to a French gardening shop the next morning to buy a packet of seeds. But my father, who was getting the garden in shape for us, refused to grow 'weeds' and threw the packet away. Now I pick wild dandelion leaves, particularly in Spring, before they become bitter.

HERBS

It is said that women often become creative and addictive gardeners in their middle age. The theory is that when they stop creating children, some females feel the need to go on to create something else.

While I am certainly no Vita Sackville-West or Rosemary Verey, it is true that in my fortieth year I suddenly developed a deep interest in herbs, and I now have an extremely pretty and very productive herb garden. Herbs are essential for healthy cooking. With less salt, fat and sugar to intensify flavours, herbs come into their own.

Almost any small area will do for a herb garden. We pulled down an ugly asbestos garage at our home in the Cotswolds, and dug up the asphalt approach. The low stone walls of this sunny corner provide a natural setting, made prettier by the ferns and other wall plants growing there. Herbs bring surprise and interest to otherwise dull foods. If you don't have outdoor space,

most herbs can be grown in pots in the kitchen or in window-boxes. The herbs most suitable for window-boxes are these small ones, which will also grow in pots: basil, chives, chervil, parsley, marjoram and thyme. Larger herbs, like borage, fennel and sage, will grow in pots, too, but will be smaller than those cultivated in a garden. Herbs which have wandering root systems, like tarragon, lemon balm and mint, grow in pots, too, but should be kept on their own as they will overrun other herbs in the same pot. A bay tree flourishes in a pot of rich soil. Most good supermarkets now stock a good range.

These are the herbs I decided to grow:

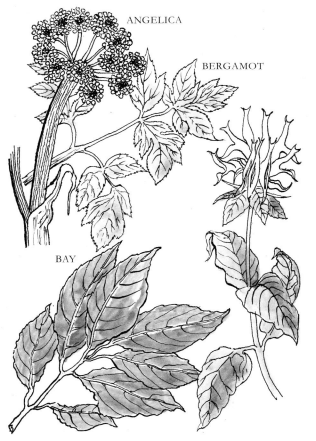

ANGELICA

BERGAMOT

BAY

ANGELICA adds style to one corner of my formal, permanent herb garden with its huge leaves and pale-green flower heads. The stalks can be boiled and candied to use for pudding decorations.

BASIL has a strong, pungent flavour which is particularly useful with tomato dishes, and in salads. It is very tender, and usually has to be grown indoors. If my seeds fail, I buy a pot from my greengrocer to keep by me in the kitchen.

BAY is essential for its useful evergreen leaves. It is used in bouquet garni and marinades.

BERGAMOT is grown for its flowers, and for its leaves to make tea.

BORAGE self-seeds all over the herb garden and has become a real pest. But it is worth all the work, for its exquisite flowers, which I use regularly for decorating salads, main courses and especially puddings. The leaves, which I use far less, have a cucumber flavour.

CHERVIL is an annual with a delicate flavour and appearance. Use like parsley.

CHIVES are very useful onion-flavoured leaves, which are excellent in potato, leek, tomato and egg

CHIVES

FENNEL

HORSERADISH

HYSSOP

recipes. The pinky, purple flowers, which appear in summer, and last a long time, improve the appearance of many dishes.

CORIANDER grows among the annuals, and I love it for its strong, lemony taste. Good with spicy, Indian dishes, and a pretty garnish.

DILL is another annual which is extremely attractive for decorating food. It is perfect with fish.

FENNEL looks pretty at the back of a herb garden, or mixed up with herbaceous plants. I grow both the green and bronze varieties. The aniseed flavour is ideal with fish.

HORSERADISH needs good soil to grow in usable pieces. It looks just like dock, and thrives on the common ground in front of our home. But we also grow some among our vegetables, and regularly use a horse-radish and yoghurt sauce with fish dishes.

HYSSOP is an attractive herb with a memorable blue flower. It is particularly good with rabbit.

LEMON BALM will grow anywhere, in both its green and variegated form. It tastes and smells strongly of lemon, and should be used sparingly. A pretty garnish.

LOVAGE is one of my favourite herbs. I use it regularly for its strong, celery-type taste with carrots, in a guinea-foul and lime dish, and in salads.

MARJORAMS grow easily and improve the appearance of herb gardens. I like them with tomatoes, courgettes, and Italian recipes.

MINTS are particularly useful, from humbly adding flavour to new potatoes, to using in the most exotic garnishes. I like apple mint for mint sauces and jellies, but there are said to be twenty-five varieties, including ginger mint and pineapple mint. Middle Eastern recipes often need mint.

NASTURTIUM is grown in both my annual herb border and among my flower beds. I use the leaves, buds, flowers and seeds, and love their peppery taste and cheerful appearance. The whole plant is full of Vitamin C.

NASTURTIUM

PARSLEY is used to edge the annual herb bed, and I usually set two lots of seeds a year, one in spring and one in the summer, so that I have a good supply through the year.

POT MARIGOLD is useful for its pretty yellow and orange petals, which can be used in rice and omelettes, as well as the more obvious salads and puddings.

ROSEMARY along with a bay tree and a sage bush, form the focal points of my formal herb garden. It is a useful evergreen herb, with lamb and chicken, but should be used in moderation as it is very strong.

SAGE is grown in both its green and red forms. The strongly scented leaves are useful with game and pork. The bright-blue flowers in summer are extremely pretty.

SALAD BURNET grows like a weed in my garden, throughout the year. The cucumber-flavoured leaves make an unusual garnish, and they can be chopped to flavour soups, stews and vinegars.

SAVORY can be used like thyme, and is excellent with bean recipes. Winter savory grows with the permanent herbs, while summer savory is an annual.

SCENTED GERANIUMS are grown for their leaves, and my favourite is the lemon-scented type. I keep it in the house in the winter, and pinch the leaves when I pass it. There are others which give off the scents of rose, mint, apple and balsam. They can be used to flavour syrups used in puddings, and to make ice-cream.

SORREL looks a little like spinach, but the flavour is much sharper. I use it in salads, sauces, and in a favourite spicy soup.

SWEET CICELY is an extremely pretty herb with bright fern-like leaves and cream flowers. These produce large black seed pods, which have a sweet aniseed flavour in salads. The leaves add sweetness to syrups being used for puddings, and they also make a beautiful garnish for fruit dishes. The leaves can be cooked with gooseberries and rhubarb to reduce their sour taste.

TARRAGON is an essential herb, again with an aniseed taste. But in this case its flavour is perfect with chicken and fish. It is a subtle herb for souffles and salads, and also makes a useful vinegar. Always grow the French variety in a sunny spot.

THYME is extremely useful in the kitchen, particularly lemon thyme and common thyme. A sprig is essential in a bouquet garni. It dries well.

POT MARIGOLD

SALAD BURNET

SAVORY

SCENTED GERANIUMS

SWEET CICELY

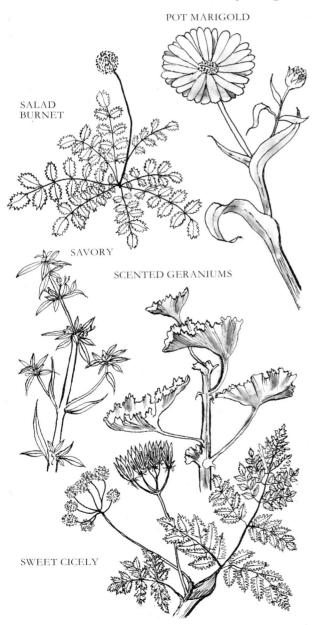

TARRAGON

FLOWERS FOR BLOSSOMING COOKS

As my confidence as a cook has blossomed, so has the range of flowers used in my food. And although they are chosen mainly for their decorative qualities, I do prefer to use flowers for garnish which are also edible.

Elderflowers were my first choice, used about 20 years ago for adding their wonderful flavour to gooseberry fool. I also use meadowsweet in a summer pudding with fresh apricots; and these delicate flowers always garnish the dish too.

My favourite has to be the borage flower. The herb itself is rather ugly and too prolific, but I will forgive it for seeding itself all over my garden, because of its exquisite flowers. They are so delicate, and such a beautiful blue with a hint of purple.

Their faint flavour of cucumber makes them a perfect addition to summer drinks, like Pimms, to crisp cucumber and lettuce salads, and to cucumber mousses and soups. But most of all I like them to garnish food of their own colour, served on Victorian blue and white china. One perfect example is my black currant cheesecake (see page 97), or kidneys served with black currant sauce (see page 86).

The cheerful lavender-pink chive flowers are also very welcome in my kitchen. They can, of course, garnish any of the many recipes using chives, including herb souffles, and they look so pretty on the beetroot creams (see page 68) and with olive flowers (see page 28). Or try a chive omelette, with a pinch of chopped chives and several flowers, for flavour and style.

I also grow marigolds in my garden, so that I can use the petals in my salads. But I have never used them for their most common purpose. Dried petals can be used as a substitute for saffron, to turn food yellow, and they are often added to stews. I prefer them for their own colour and freshness, so I scatter them on salads when the colour is helpful.

Nasturtium flowers, buds and leaves are all useful for their peppery taste and their good looks. The cheerful, delicate flowers have been used as edible decoration since the plant arrived from Peru in the 17th century. They have been forgotten as a food for a very long time, but in the 80's they have made a comeback. They are sold in the salad departments of some supermarkets these days. The flowers or young leaves can be used alone in a bitter salad, but I prefer to mix them with other salad stuffs, as you will see in my mangetout, carrot and orange salad (see page 68), and in my dish where quail is served on mixed salad leaves (see page 114). When anything orange is being used, such as julienne of carrot, a nasturtium flower often balances the food arrangement beautifully.

Geranium leaves, blackcurrant leaves and sweet cicely can be used to give a lovely scent and taste to the syrup used in water ices, cooked fruit, and coulis. But I have never used the flowers.

Any herb in flower is useful to garnish a dish, which has been cooked with the herb. It neatly labels the flavour for the people lucky enough to be eating your food. Marjoram, thyme, sage, salad burnet, hyssop and many others regularly decorate, as well as flavour, the food at my table.

And roses, of course, must never be forgotten. Old-fashioned varieties are best when making crystallized rose petals. Pick them early in the morning, cut away the white base, which is bitter, rinse and dry. Dip in beaten egg-white and castor sugar, and dry very slowly, over a boiler or in a very low oven. Other flowers which can be crystallized include borage, violet, and wood anemonies. Leaves like mint can be treated in the same way. Use them all to decorate puddings and ices.

There is no doubt about it, flowers are the perfect ingredient for the food of love.

PRESENTATION

Cooking has just been formally accepted as one of the arts in France, and I think deservedly so. Food should not only be cooked well, it should also be artistically presented. Food is so often ruined by its poor appearance. I use a mixture of modern and antique plates, and have a particular weakness for large white plates and Victorian blue and white china, which enrich the colour of herbs.

Old Victorian moulds produce glamorous wine jellies and vegetable cakes, while individual ring moulds are useful for cucumber or tomato mousse filled with sea-food.

Salads in particular can be made to look special with so many relatively new ingredients easily available. Radiccio is on sale, along with oak leaf lettuce, lamb's lettuce and edible flowers like nasturtium. And for puddings, frost leaves and flowers with egg-white and sugar, using violets, roses, mint leaves or fruits like grapes, strawberries and greengages. Or dip fruits in sugar syrup and glaze puddings with apricot or red currant jelly.

Attractive food whets the appetite, and makes people feel special. So garnish food artistically, whenever possible, in some of the following ways:

Vegetables can be used to decorate individual plates of food, or main serving dishes. Mange-tout and stick beans can be fanned; individual portions of vegetables can be tied into bunches with chives; or a range of five or six different vegetables can be arranged prettily on each side-plate. Slices of vegetable terrine in three colours, like my recipe on page 112, look exquisite. And even boiled potatoes can look great, wrapped prettily with chives.

It is really just a question of using your imagination. Red, yellow, green and even black peppers can be halved and used to serve vegetable soups. Spinach can be blanched and then wrapped round vegetables to make parcels; and sprouted seeds, grown in the kitchen, can be added to stir-fried vegetables and salads of all kinds. I think that the thing to avoid is over-complicated vegetable dishes. If you are eating a main course with a sauce, the sort of mixed vegetables served by some restaurants, including *ratatouille*, spinach in a cream sauce and so on, are totally inappropriate. Vegetables should look pretty, and be crisp and fresh, but unless they are eaten with plain food, their taste should be simple.

There are too many ideas to include here. But try making a mushroom pâté to add to vegetable mixtures, to stuff tomatoes and to flavour soups and sauces. Cook whole perfect mushrooms in wine vinegar and spices, to keep as a tasty garnish. Steam shredded white cabbage and leeks together for a simple, but subtle vegetable. Try a julienne of celery and potato, or make mixed-vegetable kebabs. Fruit and vegetables often mix, so try pears with potatoes. When you are having a simple meal, try tossing cooked swede with chopped watercress and *fromage blanc*. Put cinnamon with parsnips, or add nutmeg and almonds to cooked brussel sprouts. Poussins and small game look interesting served on a nest of potatoes. *Rosti*, the Swiss way of serving potatoes, is excellent: parboil the potatoes, slice, drench in garlic and margarine and cook until crisp.

OLIVES can be cut into five sections, when the stone is being removed, to form a flower-like garnish for pizzas, salads and pâtés. Put a chive flower in the centre of a black olive flower garnish, so it looks as if it forms the stamens.

SPRING ONION TASSELS are made simply from 2 to 4 inch pieces. Cut through the stalk a few times to half-way down the piece. When they are put in chilled water for an hour or two, they open out attractively. The same effect is achieved with celery pieces of 2 or 3 inches long.

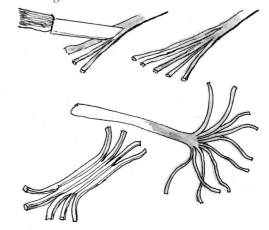

TURNED MUSHROOMS should garnish mushroom dishes, like mushroom quiche, to give a hint of what is in the recipe. Start with firm button mushrooms and run a sharp knife from the centre of the cap to the edge, to remove a little flesh. Cook in the normal way.

TOMATO ROSES are made by removing the skin in one long strip about $\frac{1}{3}$ inch wide. Curl up to form a flower with the flesh side inside. These can be used to garnish many foods, especially salads. They can be grouped into a flower on stalks using chives.

JULIENNE VEGETABLES Although I have a special disc for my food processor which is supposed to produce these vegetable strips, I prepare them by hand because the disc produces strips which are too fine. I have never discovered anything else that can cut them the correct size.

Use carrot, fennel, turnip, celeriac, kohlrabi, courgettes, peppers and potato. Peel and slice the vegetables into strips about $\frac{1}{8}$ inch wide and about $1\frac{1}{2}$ inches long.

AN ANCHOVY LATTICE looks elegant on tomato salads and egg dishes. Soak the anchovy fillets in milk for half an hour. Dry and cut into thin strips, ready to form the design.

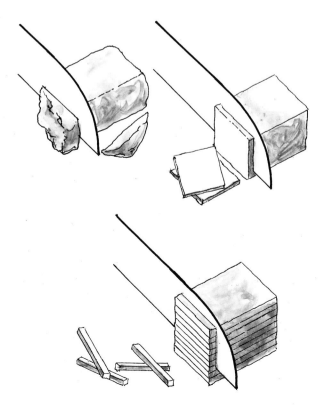

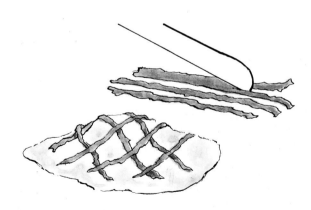

EGG-WHITE GARNISH
Cooked egg-white, transformed into exotic shapes with aspic cutters, looks elegant floating in soups or sitting in salads. Make this garnish by whisking an egg-white with 2 tablespoons of milk and a little pepper. Bake in a cocotte for eight minutes. When cold, turn out and cut into heart or diamond shapes. Float in soups just before serving.

LIME, LEMON AND ORANGE GARNISHES

A gadget called a canelle knife will not only remove fine strips of skin for garnish, it will also produce attractive designs on the skin before the fruit is cut for other decorations.

Holding the fruit, use the knife to remove strips of skin at regular intervals (drawing 1). Cut into extremely thin slices (2). These can be used for a garnish. A lime slice looks attractive lying on top of a larger lemon or orange slice.

The slice can also be cut from the edge to the centre and twisted into a cone (3), or the slices can be cut in half and then the halves cut almost into the centre before being opened out to form a butterfly (4). All of these designs can also be made using cucumber slices.

Fruit segments are needed for many puddings and salads, as well as for garnishing fish, duck and chicken. They are made by cutting a slice from the top and bottom of the fruit, then the skin plus pith is cut away from the sides. The next part demands a very sharp knife because you have to cut between the membranes to remove each segment, so the fruit is completely clear of pith and membrane.

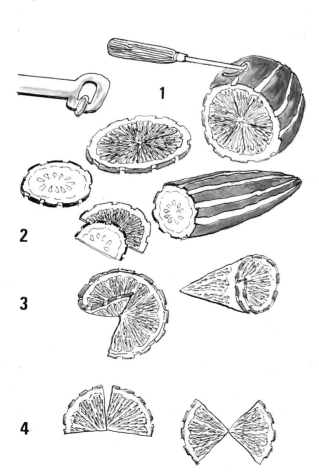

JULIENNE FRUITS

These can be made in the same way as julienne vegetables, with the peel of orange, lime, lemon and grapefruit. Blanch for one minute. A canelle knife can also be bought to remove the peel in thin strips, instead of using a knife. If you are lucky, the skin will come off in one long piece, which will be useful as a spiral to decorate poached pears.

FRUIT BASKET

These can be made from melons, pineapples, oranges, lemons, grapefruits, kiwi fruits and even tomatoes, to hold fruit mixes, sorbets, souffles and salads. They can be cut with handles, although I think these look twee. I prefer to see the smaller fruits cut simply in half, or with zigzags. Larger fruit, like melons and pineapples, can have their lids replaced at a slight angle, so the contents are revealed.

STARTLING STARTERS

The starter is my first love, and I get the greatest pleasure from preparing this part of a meal. It is so easy to make starters look special: on individual plates, using all the tricks you know to make your guests feel loved and spoilt through the food you are serving. The pâté can be dressed with olive flowers (see page 28), the tomatoes with anchovy lattice (see page 29); while aspic, herbs, moulds and vegetable cases can be used to present a tasty, healthy start to the meal.

I have always enjoyed making good soups. As I boil up a carcass for stock, chop up the vegetables, and purée the end result, I usually feel rather worthy and housewifely. Soups can be made with almost every type of vegetable. Tomato soup is a favourite in my house. Using the basic recipe for tomato sauce (see page 19), I add stock to make a basic soup, and often serve plain tomato soup with yoghurt and chives; tomato and orange soup; Latin American spicy soup, with the addition of red capsicum and a red chilli; and tomato soup with basil. Jerusalem artichoke soup, made simply with one pound of these ugly, but delicious, roots, and one onion and stock, is a family favourite. Soups can, of course, be far more special and a lot more surprising: a wild nettle soup in the spring (see page 37); a Turkish cucumber soup flavoured with mint, garlic and yoghurt (see page 104); or a successful combination of sorrel and Indian spices (see page 70). Liven up a soup with some healthy *croûtons*. These can be made by cubing wholemeal bread, coating the cubes in crushed garlic and baking in a medium oven for 10 minutes.

Pâtés and terrines can be fatty and far from healthy, but there are many recipes which can be used without breaking the rules. I love a rabbit terrine made with nuts. I make several fish terrines; a chicken and herb terrine looks very special, and my pheasant pâté (see page 116) is famous among my friends.

HEALTHY MAIN COURSES

The health message here is to reduce the quantity of meat eaten, and to use ingredients lower in fat, like game, chicken, turkey, offal, leaner cuts of meat like fillet of lamb and pork, and, of course, fish. All this is easy for me because they happen to be the foods I enjoy most. I like the strong tastes of offal; chicken goes so well with many different flavours; and game is special enough for any perfect meal.

FISH

There is one very simple way to improve your health, and that is to eat more fish. Just one or two fresh fish meals a week will be enough to dramatically decrease your chances of having a heart attack, or suffering from the effects of a blood clot. The oily fish, including mackerel, salmon, sprats, herrings, sea trout and sardines, are particulalry healthy, because they contain certain polyunsaturated fats which are far more effective than the polyunsaturates in vegetable oils and vegetables. They lower the levels of substances in the blood which block our arteries and encourage blood clots to form.

White fish is less effective in this way, but it is also healthy because it is low in the damaging saturated fats. The Japanese, who eat far more fish than we do, and who eat very little red meat and dairy products, live on average seventeen years longer than we do in the West. Although we do eat far too little fresh fish, the situation is improving.

Mackerel is meaty and versatile. I've cooked it with bacon, or apples, grilled it under a coating of home-made tartare sauce as well as served it traditionally with gooseberries. When I first went back to an office after years of being at home with the children, my husband dipped into Claudia Rodin's excellent book on Middle Eastern food to produce a new one to me – mackerel stuffed with stuffed dates. But thanks to an ill-chosen lunch in the BBC canteen I came home green, and the rich smells drove me straight to bed even greener. My version of this recipe is on page 48 – it's rich but very good.

MEAT

Nick Gill, the talented chef who made a name for himself at Hambleton Hall, has told me that his customers now ask for more fish dishes than meat. In fact, the sales of beef, lamb and pork have dropped since we have all been warned to eat less red meat. But it is still possible to eat the leaner cuts, and I use pork and lamb fillet fairly regularly. I also like the best-end neck of lamb – always asking my butcher to remove as much fat as possible. One of my favourite recipes is lemon-stuffed lamb (see page 52).

GAME

Game is particularly healthy. Lean people need a diet to match. And for meat-eaters that means game, because wild animals are leaner and fitter than farm-reared animals. Game tastes richer and stronger because fit muscle fibres contain more pigment, and because these animals eat a more varied diet. Wild animals, because they are strong and fit, contain less saturated fat and more polyunsaturates than domesticated animals, which are flabby and unfit.

If you like game, spread the word around, because some people who have access to it are less keen. For example, we discovered that a local farmer threw away all the pigeons he shot because no one in his family likes the taste. One friend, who shoots a lot of rabbits, regularly leaves a couple by the back door (which a fox got to first on one occasion). And we are given pheasant, wild duck and hare by people who just cannot be bothered to pluck or skin them themselves.

HEALTHY PUDDINGS

The best of healthy puddings are those which are delicate in taste but rich in colour. It is particularly important that puddings look good. The finale to the perfect meal should definitely have an 'Ah!' factor.

Garnishes are, therefore, very useful, and I have included dozens of exotic ideas on presenting food. Many people do not realize that several herbs are ideal for garnishing puddings, and even for flavouring the syrups that form the basis of some dishes. I regularly use mint, sweet cicely, geranium leaves, and the leaves of the black currant. Edible flowers, like violet, rose petals, borage and nasturtium, can make puddings look very special.

Many people ask me how I can possibly serve extravagant, exquisite puddings without using rich pastry and double cream. Well, pastry does not feature regu-larly in my cooking, although I do find it worthwhile to make some special fruit flans with wholemeal pastry. And even the unhealthiest of traditional puddings can be modified. For example, one of my favourites is a cheesecake made, not with rich cheese and half a pint of double cream, but with 1 lb/450 g of *fromage blanc* to replace those two unhealthy ingredients. The final result is much less heavy, and is preferred by everyone who has tried it.

I do normally like light puddings served in small quantities, be it papaya with lime and tequila, or one of my favourite sorbets or yoghurt-based ice-creams. But the most important pudding ingredients in my kitchen are definitely local fruits, picked in season and enjoyed at their freshest and tastiest.

A HEALTHY CHEESEBOARD

I make cheeses happy in the knowledge that my own home-made versions contain no additives and virtually no fat. It is not easy when buying cheese, because some of the world's best and tastiest cheeses are high in salt, fats and preservatives. Two-thirds of the cheese eaten in this country, for example, is Cheddar. We spend almost £500 million on this cheese alone. Although it contains important minerals and vitamins, it is alarmingly high in saturated fats. In fact it is one-third fat, which is why so many manufacturers have been concentrating on making and selling Cheddar cheeses which are lower in fat. I find that few of these have a good taste, but one of the best for flavour is Sainsbury's, with 14 per cent fat. Dairycare's Cheddar, at 22.5 per cent fat, has a strong flavour, so less is needed in sauces.

Roquefort, Danish Blue and Parmesan are 29 per cent fat, 18 per cent saturated. Edam and Gouda are perhaps the healthiest of the traditional hard cheeses, at 23 per cent fat, but do ask at your cheese shop, because new cheeses are now being made from skimmed milk, like the Berkeley I mention later. Brie and Camembert are 23 per cent fat; curd cheese is normally about 10 per cent; cottage cheese just over 4 per cent; while *fromage blanc* has less than 2 per cent, and often no fat at all. But when you buy these so-called 'healthy' low-fat cheeses, check for additives on the label, because some of them contain far too many for comfort.

I am not very fond of cottage cheese, but if you like it, Loseley make an excellent one for flavour, with just over 4 per cent fat.

However, it is possible to produce an interesting and inspiring cheeseboard without breaking any health rules, and it is getting easier as manufacturers begin to produce more cheeses made from skimmed milk and other low-fat ingredients. Perhaps if I describe my latest cheeseboard, it will help to give you some ideas. When I went to look at my local cheese shop I discovered that they stocked several low-fat offerings, and I chose one smooth cheese made from Roquefort and *fromage blanc*, and an orange, marbled cheese made from skimmed milk, called Berkeley. I then added these two low-fat cheeses.

Basil and walnut cheese

4 oz/100 g curd cheese or *fromage blanc*
2 tbsp fresh basil, finely chopped
2 oz/50 g walnuts, pound half and finely chop the other half
1 leaf fresh basil for garnish
pepper

Mix the curd cheese with the chopped basil, pepper and pounded walnuts. Then roll the mixture in the chopped walnuts. Decorate the finished cheese with a basil leaf and half a walnut.

Herb cheese

1 lb/450 g *fromage blanc* or home-made curd cheese
2 tbsp sunflower oil
4 tbsp finely chopped mixed chervil, tarragon and parsley
2 cloves garlic creamed with very little salt
lots of freshly ground pepper

Mix all ingredients well, and put into pierced heart-shaped moulds. Leave for several hours, and then turn out on to fresh vine leaves or a bed of herbs to serve. Although this can be served as a first course, I usually leave it until later in the meal to add to other cheeses.

The cheeses were arranged on a huge platter with spring onion tassels (see page 28), radish waterlillies and celery stalks (see page 30) with black grapes, clementines , and the following oat biscuits made with small heart-shaped biscuit cutters.

Oat biscuits

6 oz/175 g medium oatmeal
4 oz/100 g wholemeal flour
dark chilli powder
1 tsp baking-powder
2 oz/50 g margarine

Mix the flour, oatmeal and baking-powder in a bowl. Then mix in the melted margarine and a small amount of hot water, until the dough is of the ideal consistency. Knead a little. Then when it feels firm, roll it out on a floured surface. Sprinkle the surface of the mixture with chilli powder (to taste) and cut out heart-shaped biscuits. Bake in a hot over for 10 to 15 minutes.

SEASONAL RECIPES

SPRING

As winter comes to an end, it is natural to want light, refreshing and healthy food, like fish, chicken and young, seasonal vegetables. And fortunately spring can provide all three. Chicken is at its best during these three months. I find it hard to remember that chicken was once a luxury food. Now it is cheap and readily available, but it is worth seeking out the unfrozen, free-range, farm-bred birds. Chicken is so useful to keen cooks, because it mixes well with a variety of different tastes, from subtle asparagus to strong, spicy Indian flavours. Poussins are pretty, but lack the flavour of bigger birds, so I normally use chicken breasts for individual portions, or large 4 lb whole birds that have plenty of taste. The carcass is always used for stock.

Spring is also an excellent time to buy oily, healthy fish like herrings, luxury items like salmon, and our family favourite, crab. They can all be served with sauces made from the new season's herbs like sorrel and fennel. I use salmon raw and marinaded, cooked traditionally, and made into a subtle mousse. And crab is enjoyed by us all, in almost every possible way. Plain crab served on a lettuce heart with tomato and avocado sauces (see page 40) is refreshing, while Nick Gill taught me a clever way of wrapping white crab meat in spinach parcels, which are then gently steamed and served with a simple sauce of brown crab meat blended with lemon juice and pepper.

Early spring is the perfect time of the year to start looking in fields, woods and hedgerows for food that is free. All edible plants are best picked young. And tender, new shoots begin to appear from March onwards. There are various rules to remember if you are thinking of joining the increasing ranks of people who look for food in the countryside. First, do make sure that you identify every plant *correctly*. Secondly, do your picking in the 'real' countryside and not from parks where hundreds of dogs are exercised, or from the sides of busy roads, where plants could be covered in traffic fumes or weedkillers. Finally, please don't ruin the countryside by picking plants too greedily: leave some for other people's eyes and stomachs.

One of the easiest ways to learn about plants and recipes to use them in is too look up old books, published at a time when we relied far more on wild varieties in our cooking.

In April, the first English lamb appears in the shops. It is expensive at this time, but is certainly at its best. I love the best end of neck of lamb stuffed with nuts and lemon (see page 52), or apricots and fennel. Or crown roast of lamb (see page 50) is perhaps the most glamorous way of serving this meat, with cutlet frills or small onions decorating the crown.

And, of course, spring brings the early vegetable harvest, the first, tiny and tender crops which should always be cooked with extra tender loving care, so that their youth and flavour emerge. Try steaming these perfect new vegetables – baby carrots, mange-tout, asparagus and spinach – using either the Chinese stacking wicker steamers, the large British type with three compartments, or the gadget like a metal flower with petals which open wide. All produce excellent results.

STARTERS

Nettle soup

I usually make this soup between April and June, when nettles are at their freshest, and before the leaves become coarse and bitter. The soup is full of healthy iron and it has an intriguing taste. But the main reason for this soup is the fun I get from making it, and the surprise for the eaters. It is always interesting to taste food which grows in the hedgerows, particularly when it is made from such a humble plant. The first time I made it, I had to do all the preparations in secret because I suspected that my two sons would not eat the soup if they knew its origins. I need not have worried. 'My 'vegetable soup' was an instant success. Nettle soup is now a family favourite.

1 large onion
1 clove garlic
1 large potato
2 tbsp oil
pepper
8 oz/225 g nettle tops
1 pt/600 ml chicken stock

Soften the finely chopped vegetables in the oil for 5 minutes. Add the washed nettle tops. (Collect these with gloves on and pull the leaves off the stalks.) Simmer in the chicken stock for about 10 minutes, or until the potatoes are cooked. Liquidize and serve with swirls of thick yoghurt, and *croûtons* (see page 31).

Vichyssoise

3 large leeks
2 potatoes
2 tbsp oil
1½ pt/900 ml chicken stock
½ pt/300 ml milk
4 oz/100 g thick yoghurt
1 tbsp chopped chives

Chop the leeks finely and dice the potatoes, and cook them gently in the oil. Add the stock and pepper. Simmer for 30 minutes, then purée. Return to the pan and add the milk, yoghurt and chives when cold. Serve very cold.

Spinach soup

8 oz/225 g older outer leaves spinach
1 onion, chopped
1 clove garlic
1 tbsp oil
1½ pt/900 ml stock
croûtons
plain yoghurt
pepper
a little nutmeg

Cook the chopped onion and garlic in oil. Then add the chopped spinach leaves, pepper and nutmeg, and simmer in stock for 20 minutes. Purée and serve well-seasoned, with wholemeal *croûtons* and a swirl of yoghurt in each bowl.

Walnut and artichoke treat

12 even-sized Jerusalem artichokes, as smooth as
   you can find
12 small shallots
4 oz/100 g walnuts, chopped
3 tbsp walnut oil
2 tbsp chopped parsley
1 tsp sugar
pepper

Peel the artichokes and put in water until the shallots are also peeled. Ideally the two sorts of vegetables should be about the same size. Boil briefly until only just tender. Heat the oil. Turn the drained vegetables in the oil until they take on a little colour. Add the chopped nuts, seasoning and half the parsley. Turn in the oil, and when hot serve with the rest of the parsley as garnish. This is a very tasty and aromatic first course for spring and winter months.

Crudités with avocado dip and aïoli

Crudités can be served through the year, although the time when the first young vegetables of the season are available is most perfect. There is a wide range of vegetables to choose from, including cauliflower sprigs, carrot, fennel, cucumber, peppers, white and red radish, celery, and broccoli. There are many dips which can be made, but I like the following two. The texture of the avocado dip is excellent, and more tabasco can be added to make it spicier. Aïoli is smelly because of all the raw garlic. But this potent clove is ultra-healthy.

AVOCADO DIP
2 large ripe avocados
1 tbsp oil
2 or 3 drops tabasco (or more to taste)
juice of 1 lemon
pepper
2 cloves garlic, crushed
chervil or parsley to garnish

Liquidize, chill and serve with the garnish.

AÏOLI
16 cloves garlic
2 egg yolks
up to ½ pt/300 ml olive oil
juice of 1 lemon
pepper

Crush the garlic to a paste and blend in the egg yolks (I use a food-processor for this). Then gradually add the olive oil to the mixture, drop by drop, mixing all the time. It should end up a good firm consistency. Season to taste with pepper and lemon juice. Arrange the crudités artistically on a large oval dish, strewn with fresh herbs, with two pots of dips in the centre.

Spinach salad with Stilton and garlic croûtons

Although spinach is available all year, it is at its best in March and April. I also serve a cold spinach leaf salad, with hot *croûtons* (see page 31), hot lean bacon cubes, and a dressing.

10 oz/275 g small spinach leaves
4 oz/100 g bread, cut into cubes
1 clove garlic, crushed
2 oz /50 g Stilton cheese, crushed
1 tbsp lemon juice
$\frac{1}{2}$ tsp French mustard
2 tbsp chopped mixed herbs
6 oz/175 g low-fat, natural yoghurt
pepper

Wash the spinach, remove the main stalks and dry. Bake the bread cubes in a medium oven for 10 minutes, and then mix in a bowl with the crushed garlic. Mix the yoghurt, mustard, lemon juice, pepper and crushed Stilton. Put the spinach in the bowl. Pour over the yoghurt-based dressing and herbs. Mix, add the *croûtons* and serve immediately.

Heart of crab with avocado and tomato sauces

8 oz/225 g fresh crab meat*
1 crisp lettuce, shredded
4 spring onions, 2 chopped and 2 made into tassels (see page 28)
AVOCADO SAUCE
1 ripe avocado
4 oz/100 g thick, plain yoghurt
lemon or lime juice to taste (1 fruit is about right)
pepper
pinch of cayenne pepper
TOMATO SAUCE
2 oz/50 g yoghurt
6 tbsp tomato pulp
tabasco to flavour (I like about 6 drops)
$\frac{1}{2}$ tbsp lemon juice

Serve this dish in the shape of a heart on individual white plates. Arrange the shredded lettuce and chopped spring onions in 4 heart-shapes. Pile the mixed brown and white crab meat in the centre, seasoned with black pepper, lemon or lime juice and a pinch of cayenne. Garnish with spring onion tassels and lime slices. Pipe the avocado sauce in a heart shape around the lettuce, followed by an outer heart of spicy tomato sauce. *Photograph on page 42.*

*Dressed crab is readily available today. However, if you want to cook and dress a live crab, here's what to do:

1 Weigh the crab and cook in boiling, salted water along with 1 bay-leaf, 5 peppercorns, 1 sliced onion, and 2 sticks of celery. Allow 15 minutes for the first 1 lb/450 g and 8 minutes for each additional 1 lb/450 g. When cooked, take the crab from the pan and allow to cool.
2 Place the crab on its back and remove the legs and claws. Set them aside.
3 To separate the body, place the tail flap towards you. Hold the shell with your fingers and, using your thumbs, push the body upwards until it is loosened and separates from the shell.
4 Take out and throw away the stomach sac and the grey gills, known as 'dead man's fingers'.
5 Spoon out the brown meat from the shell and put in a bowl.
6 Cut the body in half and dig out the white meat from all the crevices. Put in a separate bowl.
7 Crack open the claws and legs. Remove all the white meat and add it to the other white meat.
8 Finely chop the white meat and season to taste.
9 Mix the brown meat and season to taste.
10 Mix the brown and white meat together.

Page 42
Heart of crab with avocado
and tomato sauces

Cucumber and prawn mousse

These look beautiful made in small, circular ring moulds. This quantity will make 4.

6 oz/175 g peeled prawns
½ cucumber
1 small packet gelatine
2 tbsp lemon juice
4 oz/100 g *fromage blanc*
cayenne pepper
fennel or dill to garnish

Soften the gelatine in the lemon juice and warm through to dissolve. Stir into this mixture half the prawns, half the cucumber (peeled and finely chopped), the pepper and the *fromage blanc*, and spoon into the oiled moulds. Chill till set. Serve garnished with the rest of the prawns and decorative cucumber and lemon slices. Serve with wholemeal bread.

Terrine of rabbit with prunes

Rabbit is improved by cooking it with hyssop, but if you do not have access to this herb, use sage instead. This terrine should be garnished with hyssop, including the flowers when they are available, and stoned prunes. *Photograph on page 43.*

1 wild rabbit, finely chopped up
8 oz/225 g prunes, soaked overnight in red wine
8 oz/225 g lean bacon, 3 oz/75 g minced, and the rest used to
layer the terrine
6 juniper berries
2 tbsp chopped hyssop or sage
pinch of mace
MARINADE
red wine
orange peel
juniper berries, crushed
6 bay-leaves
several peppercorns

Page 43
Terrine of rabbit with prunes

Put the flesh of the rabbit in a marinade overnight. Grease a 1½ pt/900 ml terrine and arrange the bay-leaves from the marinade along the bottom. Take 6 whole juniper berries, put them among the bay-leaves, and lay bacon on the bottom and sides. Then layer the rabbit with herbs and mace, followed by stoned prunes and bacon, followed by more rabbit, until the ingredients have been used up. End with a layer of bacon. Pour over the strained marinade, and cover. Cook in a medium oven by standing the terrine in a dish of hot water, for about 2 hours.

MAIN COURSES

Mullet in a parcel

Red mullet is at its best from mid-spring until late summer.

4 red mullet, cleaned
4 tbsp oil
pepper
1 root Florentine fennel
1 lemon
fennel (the herb) and lemon to garnish

Make diagonal slits in the fish, sprinkle with pepper and lemon juice, and leave coated with half the oil for an hour or two. Prepare the fennel by chopping it, blanching it for a few minutes, and then flavouring it with lemon juice and pepper. Stuff the fish with this mixture. Then cut 4 ovals of grease-proof paper, and brush with the rest of the oil. Wrap the fish up in these. Bake the parcels in a medium oven for 15 minutes and serve each one with a spring of fennel and a twist of lemon.

Spinach roulade with a spicy sauce

This vegetable roulade makes a very refreshing main course to serve on a special occasion. The dark green and cream roulade, with the red sauce, looks wonderful. *Photograph opposite.*

ROULADE

8 oz/225 g cooked, chopped spinach

2 tbsp Parmesan cheese

4 egg-whites

2 egg yolks

pepper

nutmeg, freshly grated

FILLING

4 oz/100 g onion, chopped

1 tbsp oil

6 oz/175 g *fromage blanc*

pepper

nutmeg

SPICY SAUCE

1 lb/450 g ripe tomatoes

1 onion, finely chopped

1 clove garlic, finely chopped

$\frac{1}{4}$ pt/150 ml chicken stock

1 tbsp oil

1 tsp of basil or marjoram

2 tbsp tomato purée

tabasco to taste

pepper

Make the sauce by peeling and chopping the tomatoes. Soften the onion, and then the garlic in the hot oil, and after a few minutes add the tomatoes. Simmer for 15 minutes with the stock, herbs and tomato purée. Season with pepper and tabasco to taste.

For the roulade, line a 12 × 8 inch/30 × 20 cm Swiss roll tin with foil and grease it lightly. Blend the spinach with the egg yolks, cheese, pepper and nutmeg. Beat the egg-whites till stiff and fold into the spinach mixture. Check for seasoning. Pour into the tin, smooth it level, and put into a hot oven for 10 minutes. Leave to cool. Then spread with a stuffing made by softening the onions in the oil and mixing with the other ingredients. Roll up and serve with the spicy sauce. This is good hot or cold.

*Page 47
Spinach roulade with a spicy
sauce*

46

Mackerel stuffed with dates

4 small mackerel
8 oz/225 g fresh dates
1 tsp root ginger, grated
3 oz/75 g chopped almonds
2 tbsp cooked rice
1 tsp sugar
$\frac{1}{2}$ tsp ground cinnamon
pinch each of pepper, ground cumin and ground ginger
2 tbsp margarine
oil
1 glass of dry white wine
fresh coriander for garnish

Wash and clean the fish. Slit open each belly and remove any bones you can. Stone the dates and stuff them with a mixture of almonds, rice, root ginger, cinnamon and a pinch of pepper and ginger – all kneaded with the margarine to keep the mixture together. Rub the fish with oil, ginger and pepper. Fill with the dates. Put on foil, sprinkle with white wine, wrap up and seal the foil. Bake in a medium oven for 20 minutes, then unwrap and allow the fish to become crisp and brown. Serve garnished with coriander.

Mackerel herb crunch

This recipe and the one for mackerel in a parcel are simpler than the previous one.

4 large mackerel fillets
8 tbsp of chopped herbs, using a mixture of fresh parsley, coriander, dill, chives and possibly chervil
2 cloves garlic, chopped
2 oz/50 g walnuts, chopped
2 oz/50 g breadcrumbs
juice and finely pared skin of half a lemon
3 tbsp olive oil
fresh sprigs of herbs and lemon slices for garnish
pepper

Mix the chopped herbs, chopped nuts, chopped garlic, lemon and breadcrumbs. Season the mixture and spread over all 4 fillets. Pour over the oil and put in a dish, cover with foil, and bake in a hot oven for 20 minutes. Remove the foil for a few minutes to allow the fish to become brown and crunchy. Serve garnished with fresh sprigs of herbs, and more lemon. This is most refreshing with a salad accompaniment.

Mackerel in a parcel, with caper and herb sauce

CAPER AND HERB SAUCE

8 oz/225 g *fromage blanc*
1 tbsp tarragon (or fennel), chopped
2 tsp gherkins, chopped
1 tsp capers, chopped
**½ tsp French mustard or tarragon mustard
  if you have it**
fresh lemon juice to taste
pepper

Mix the ingredients together.

4 small mackerel, cleaned
4 bay-leaves
4 sprigs tarragon (or fennel)
4 lemon slices

Put the herbs inside the fish, with the lemon and seasoning on top. Grease 4 pieces of foil, and put the mackerel in the centre of them. Bake in a medium oven for 30 minutes. Serve with the sauce, garnished with fresh herbs and lemon.

Crown roast of lamb stuffed with fresh red currants

A crown roast is two best ends joined. Cutlet frills can be used to decorate this handsome dish, but I prefer the more unusual garnish of glazed shallots on the cutlet bones. This is a perfect dish when our spring lamb first appears in the shops. Lamb is often fatty, but the best end of lamb with its fat removed is a very acceptable special meal within a healthy regime.

1 onion, finely chopped
1 clove garlic
2 oz/50 g mushrooms, chopped
1 oz/25 g margarine
8 oz/225 g fresh, prepared red currants
½ cup parsley, chopped
1 tbsp thyme, chopped (lemon preferably)
4 oz/100 g breadcrumbs
1 egg, beaten
pepper
2 tbsp red currant jelly

Soften the onion, garlic and mushrooms in the margarine. Then add this mixture to the red currants, parsley, thyme, breadcrumbs, egg and black pepper. Mix well together and fill the crown. Wrap foil around the bones to protect them and cook for 30 minutes per pound/450 g in a hot oven. Make a sauce from the juices, with the fat removed, heated with the red currant jelly.

Page 51
Crown roast of lamb stuffed
with fresh red currants

Pork and juniper berries

1 lb/450 g pork fillet
2 oz/50 g margarine
12 juniper berries, crushed
pepper
2 glasses dry sherry

Slice the fillet across in thin sections. Flatten with a steak hammer and pepper each piece of pork, adding some crushed juniper berries. Fry on both sides in margarine for 3 minutes. Add the sherry to the juices, and serve with a green salad.

Steamed sea bass

Sea bass is a very handsome and very tasty fish, which seems to blend happily with Chinese ingredients. This is a dish which uses one of my favourite ingredients, root ginger. Thin slices of sea bass are also excellent eaten raw, after spending 24 hours marinading in a mixture of lime juice, coriander and seasoning.

1 whole sea bass of about 3 lb/1.5 kg
a bunch of spring onions
2 tbsp oil
1 glass of dry white wine
1 tbsp soy sauce
root ginger
pepper

Gut the fish, but leave whole. Slice up a 2-inch/5-cm square piece of ginger, and chop up 4 of the onions. Mix together. Put half of this mixture inside the fish, and half over the top. Coat the fish with half the oil, add some pepper and sprinkle over the wine. Steam for about 20 minutes. Then heat the rest of the oil, add a 1-inch/2.5-cm square piece of ginger, grated finely, and 6 chopped spring onions. Cook for 2 minutes. Add the soy sauce. Serve the fish with this sauce poured over it, having removed the ginger and onions used in steaming. Garnish with spring onion tassels (see page 28), and serve with rice and crisp, Chinese-style green vegetables (see page 59).

Lemon-stuffed lamb

2 lb/900 g boned, best-end neck of lamb
1 onion, finely chopped
1 clove garlic, finely chopped
1 cup breadcrumbs
grated rind and juice of 1 small lemon
1 egg, beaten
2 oz/50 g chopped nuts, preferably walnuts
1 tbsp oil
1 tbsp chopped chervil (parsley can be used instead,
  but it won't give the distinctive flavour)
wine
pepper

ACCOMPANIMENT
4 tomatoes, cut in half
lemon juice
chopped chervil
pepper

Soften the onion and garlic in the oil. Then add the lemon juice and rind, breadcrumbs, nuts, chervil, seasoning and beaten egg. Roll the lamb around the stuffing, and fasten. Pour over a little white wine and roast in a medium oven for an hour. Serve with the tomatoes, grilled for 5 minutes and flavoured with lemon juice, chopped chervil and pepper. Baby new potatoes and crisp green vegetables, sprinkled with lemon, are perfect with this dish.

Grilled lamb breasts

1 breast of lamb
2 carrots, chopped
1 onion, chopped
pinch of mixed herbs
1 lemon
seasoning
1 egg, beaten
brown breadcrumbs
ACCOMPANIMENT
caper and herb sauce (see page 49)

Place the breast of lamb in a casserole with chopped carrots, onions, herbs and seasoning. Cover with water and cook in a low oven for about 3 hours, preferably when you are cooking another dish slowly. Leave to cool, remove the fat from the top and take out the lamb. The remaining stock and vegetables should be sieved to make a delicious soup. Remove all the lean lamb, cut into strips, coat in beaten egg and brown breadcrumbs and grill for about 10 minutes, until crisp. Serve with lemon slices, caper and herb sauce, potatoes and watercress.

Chicken in a parcel with a tarragon and prawn sauce

4 chicken breasts
4 sheets of filo pastry
1 clove garlic, crushed
1 tbsp tarragon, chopped
lemon juice
2 oz/50 g margarine
oil
pepper
tarragon for garnish
SAUCE
1 tsp tarragon mustard
1 tsp tarragon, chopped
4 oz/100 g cooked prawns, chopped
2 glasses dry white wine
1 tbsp *fromage frais*
1 tsp tomato purée
1 shallot
1 tbsp oil

Prepare the chicken breasts by removing any skin, and trimming and flattening the meat. Make a herb butter by creaming together the garlic, pepper, tarragon, lemon juice and margarine. Divide into 4 and spread a portion on to each chicken breast. Roll up the breasts and fasten with a cocktail stick. Brown in the oil, cool a little, and remove the stick. Then brush the filo pastry with oil, fold each sheet in half and put a chicken breast in the centre. Pick up the 4 corners of the pastry, bring them together and twist into an attractive parcel. Bake in a medium oven for 20 minutes.

Make the sauce by softening the chopped shallot in oil, then adding the mustard, tarragon, tomato purée, prawns and wine. Simmer, and then just before serving, stir in the *fromage frais*. Put a pool of the sauce on each plate, and add a brown, crisp parcel in the centre. Garnish with tarragon, and arrange steamed mange-tout, stick beans and small broccoli spears on each plate.

Page 55
Chicken in a parcel with a
tarragon and prawn sauce

Kidneys with mustard

2 calf's kidneys
1 tbsp French mustard
4 tbsp *fromage blanc*
6 juniper berries, crushed
pepper
2 tbsp oil
1 glass brandy

Mix the mustard with the *fromage blanc*. Slice the kidneys and cover them with juniper berries, pressed well in. Season with pepper. Heat the oil, and cook the kidneys for about 5 minutes. Add a dash of brandy and the mustard mixture. Heat through and serve with spinach.

Marsala liver

1 lb/450 g of lambs' or calves' liver, thinly sliced
2 onions, finely chopped
2 cloves garlic, finely chopped
4 oz/100 g firm button mushrooms, roughly chopped
1 tsp fresh rosemary leaves, crushed
2 tsp oil
6–8 tbsp Marsala
pepper

Soak the mushrooms in the Marsala for half an hour. Soften the onions and garlic in the oil for a few minutes. Add the mushroom pieces. Cook these for 2 minutes. In a separate pan, cook the liver pieces briskly on each side until small pink droplets appear. Add the vegetable mixture, rosemary, Marsala and pepper. Cook until you have a syrupy consistency. Serve the liver with the sauce poured over, garnished with turned mushrooms (see page 29) and sprigs of rosemary. This is good with simple vegetables, like new potatoes in their skins, broccoli, French beans and crisp cauliflower.

Pork and prunes

1 pork fillet, cut horizontally into 12 circles of pork,
 and flattened with a steak hammer
6 prunes soaked in a glass of red wine
1 tbsp oil
$\frac{1}{4}$ pt/150 ml chicken stock
2 tbsp chervil, chopped
pepper
red currant jelly (optional)

Cut the soaked prunes into 4. Make 2 holes in each piece of pork, and press a piece of prune into them. Cook the pork rounds in a little oil for 3 minutes on each side. Pepper them well. Keep warm. Add stock, and the wine used with the prunes, to the pan. Cook till syrupy, then pour over the pork. Sprinkle with chopped chervil, and serve with a green vegetable. Red currant jelly can be added to the sauce to make it even richer.

Chicken with dill and vermouth sauce

4 chicken breasts
1 tbsp oil
2 fl oz/50 ml vermouth
grated rind of half a lemon
$\frac{1}{4}$ pt/150 ml chicken stock
1 tbsp dill, chopped
1 tbsp *fromage blanc*
pepper
dill and lemon for garnish

Cook the chicken breasts in the oil for a couple of minutes on both sides. When lightly cooked, keep warm, and prepare the sauce. Add all the other ingredients to the pan of chicken cooking juices, apart from the *fromage blanc*. Reduce the sauce until it is beginning to go syrupy, and then add the *fromage blanc* just before serving. Put a pool of the sauce on each plate, top it with a chicken breast, and garnish with lemon twists and dill. Serve with steamed new potatoes in their skins and a selection of crisp, green vegetables.

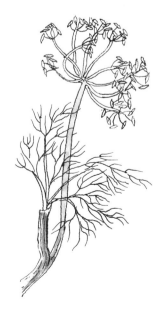

Oriental chicken

This is, if you like, a more interesting and healthier version of Chicken Kiev. It is more interesting because it is stuffed with garlic and ginger, and it is far lower in fat because it is grilled rather than deep-fried. It is a familiar favourite in my family, because it is simple, quick and yet very special. The two main tastes are root ginger and sesame oil, both ingredients which stimulate my saliva to flow as soon as their aroma fills the kitchen.

4 chicken breasts
2 fat cloves garlic
1-inch/2.5-cm square piece of root ginger
2 tbsp chopped coriander, or parsley if preferred
2 tbsp sesame oil
1 to 2 tbsp soy sauce (preferably superior soy)
pepper
herb for garnish

Finely chop the garlic and root ginger, and then soften them in half the sesame oil. Then make a slit in the chicken breasts and put a quarter of this mixture in each, with some of the chopped herb. Colour the breasts on both sides in the same oil, pepper them, pour on the rest of the oil and the soy sauce and grill the breasts on both sides. They should be served when the flesh is still succulent with the oriental sauce.

A crisp green vegetable, and new potatoes in their skins, can be served with this dish, or it can be transformed into a more special and more oriental meal by serving it with Chinese-style vegetables. Here are two suggestions:

Chinese-style vegetables

STIR-FRIED SPINACH

1 lb/450 g spinach
2 cloves garlic, crushed
2 slices root ginger, grated
4 tbsp oil
2 tbsp soy sauce
1 tbsp chicken stock

Wash the spinach; take off the large stems and tear leaves into pieces. Heat the oil in a wok and add the crushed garlic and grated ginger. After 1 minute, add the spinach, and cook for another 2 minutes. Add the other ingredients and stir quickly until the liquid has evaporated.

CHINESE CABBAGE

1 large cabbage, shredded
2 tbsp oil
$\frac{1}{2}$ pt/300 ml chicken stock
1 tbsp grated ginger
pepper
2 tsp sesame oil

Heat the oil, add the ginger for a minute, and then the shredded cabbage. Add the pepper and the stock. Cover and simmer for several minutes. Sprinkle with sesame oil and serve.

VEGETABLES

Potatoes with goat's cheese

1 lb/450 g potatoes in their skins, washed
1 clove garlic, crushed
1 shallot
1 tbsp oil
8 oz/225 g chicken or vegetable stock
4 oz/100 g goat's cheese
pepper

Cut the potatoes into thin slices, and arrange in a dish in layers, with the pepper and garlic. Soften the shallot in oil, and add with the stock. Cook in a medium oven for half an hour. Then sprinkle the goat's cheese over the top and brown under the grill.

PUDDINGS

CITRUS FRUIT PUDDINGS

Citrus fruits are excellent at this time of year, and I use even more lemons, oranges and grapefruits than usual from February through to late spring. I often keep the shells to use as baskets for sorbets and ice-creams, and occasionally I use citrus skins to crystallize as an end-of-dinner treat.

Orange and apricot creams

2 oranges
1 lb/450 g dried apricots
sugar to taste
3 tbsp Cointreau
4 oz/100 g *fromage frais*
2 oz/50 g toasted slivered almonds

Soak the apricots overnight. Add the orange flesh and half the rind, finely shredded. Simmer in water for 10 minutes. Purée and taste. Add sugar if necessary. Allow to cool. Add the Cointreau and *fromage frais*. Chill and serve in pretty glasses with the nuts scattered on top, and garnished with orange and mint.

Orange flowers

4 oranges
1 tbsp sugar
1 tsp cornflower
4 tbsp water
juice of another orange
1 tsp finely grated and blanched orange rind
3 tbsp brandy
sprigs of mint

Prepare the oranges by cutting through the skin from the stem, almost to the other side, forming 6 segments. You then curl these inwards so that they tuck in under the orange flesh at the bottom. Loosen the orange segments so that they can be eaten easily. Make the sauce by gently combining all the ingredients, apart from the mint, preferably using a double saucepan. Cool the sauce. Just before serving, coat the oranges with it, and garnish with mint. *Photograph on page 62.*

Sliced orange salad

5 ripe blood oranges
10 fresh dates
2 oz/50 g slivered almonds
2 kumquats
orange flower water
cinnamon

Peel the oranges and slice them as thinly as possible. Put them in a large, shallow dish and scatter them with chopped dates, nuts and finely sliced, unpeeled kumquats. Sprinkle over orange flower water and chill. When serving, sprinkle over the powdered cinnamon.

Pineapple and citrus ice pudding

4 slices of fresh pineapple
2 oranges, sectioned
4 scoops of pineapple sorbet
4 tbsp Kirsch
2 oz/50 g toasted slivered almonds
mint for garnish

Remove the hard centre from the pineapple slices and replace it with a scoop of sorbet. Pour 1 tbsp of Kirsch on each slice and arrange half of an orange on each, cut into sections as described on page 30. Sprinkle on the nuts and garnish with mint.

Pineapple sorbet

12 oz/350 g fresh pineapple, peeled and cored
juice of 2 lemons
4 oz/100 g sugar
1 tsp vanilla essence
$\frac{1}{2}$ pt/300 ml water
2 egg-whites
lemon and mint for garnish

Page 62
Orange flowers

Purée the pineapple. Mix in the other ingredients, except for the egg-whites. Freeze the mixture until almost frozen, (about 30 minutes). Whisk the egg-whites, fold in to the pineapple mixture, and freeze for 3 hours. This looks good served in the hollowed-out pineapple shell, garnished with lemon, thin slices of pineapple, and mint.

Orange or lemon sorbet

½ pt/300 ml water
3 oz/75 g sugar
1 egg-white
juice and zest of 3 oranges (or 3 lemons)

Finely grate the zest, and boil with the sugar in the water for 10 minutes. Add the strained fruit juice and make as above.

Grapefruit sorbet can be made with 2 fruits, as above. Finely chopped mint can be added.

ICE-CREAMS

It is normally difficult to eat ice-cream on a healthy diet, because most recipes are high in both fat and sugar. But I have found that excellent ice-creams can be made with yoghurt as the base. I make them regularly now as I have a small sorbet and ice-cream maker. But as I explain above, in the sorbet recipes, they are easy to make by hand. It is best with ice-creams to freeze the mixture until it is slushy, then to beat again and refreeze. Repeat this three times for the best results.

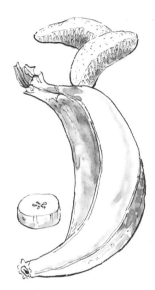

Banana ice-cream

3 ripe bananas
2 oz/50 g sugar
4 tbsp honey
¼ pt/150 ml milk
⅓ pt/200 ml plain yoghurt
juice of 2 lemons

Purée all the ingredients. Make as above in the sorbet recipes. Serve with slices of banana in lemon juice, with lemon garnish.

*Page 63
Pineapple sorbet*

Coffee and nut ice-cream

¼ pt/150 ml strong coffee
2 oz/50 g chopped hazelnuts
3 tbsp honey
4 oz/100 g plain yoghurt
¼ pt/150 ml milk

Blend together and make as above in the sorbet recipes.

64

PUDDING EXTRAS

Yoghurt snow

This recipe is extremely useful when you are missing cream. It is an excellent accompaniment to fresh fruits and most desserts.

8 oz/225 g thick, plain Greek-style yoghurt
2 egg-whites, whipped
1 oz/25 g castor sugar

Fold the stiff egg-whites and sugar into the yoghurt. Serve with desserts in place of cream. This can also be flavoured with brandy, Kirsch and many other liqueurs.

Nut curlings

It is not necessary to serve delicate, sweet biscuits with puddings. But if you do feel the need, here are two recipes.

3 oz/75 g sugar
3 oz/75 g margarine
2 oz/50 g wholemeal flour
2 oz/50 g chopped nuts, preferably hazlenuts

Cream the margarine and sugar together. Stir in the flour and nuts. Put half-teaspoonfuls of this mixture on to a greased baking tin, and flatten. Bake in a hot oven for several minutes. When light-brown, remove and curl over rolling-pins.

Almond biscuits

3 egg-whites
3 oz/75 g castor sugar
4 oz/100 g ground almonds
almond halves

Whisk the egg-whites, add the sugar slowly and then fold in the ground almonds. Pipe a little on to baking sheets. Add an almond half to each and bake in a medium oven for about 20 minutes.

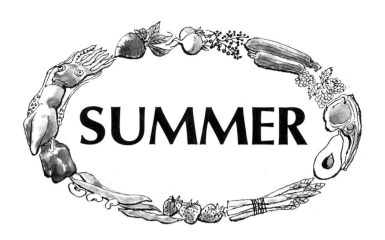

SUMMER

Summer is the highlight of a cook's year, because there is the widest variety of ingredients. Herbs are at their best, edible flowers are growing in the garden, and it becomes difficult to choose between all the vegetables on offer. And, of course, local strawberries and raspberries become available. It is even possible to find the small, wild strawberries that taste so sweet. Home-grown or farm-picked fruits taste so much better than most on sale in shops, because they should be eaten as quickly as possible after harvesting. And do not turn your noise up at the cheaper, over-ripe 'jam' strawberries and raspberries. They are often sharper in flavour than the solid, newer fruits, and are perfect for many recipes.

As well as the soft, red fruits, I look forward to the peaches, gooseberries, apricots and cherries of summer. And although this is often the time to serve fruit straight with cream, it is possible to make sure you don't miss cream too much by making delicious yoghurt snow (see page 65) to accompany puddings.

I also love the tiny courgettes with their flowers during the summer, as well as squash, baby beetroots, broad beans, new potatoes, flavoursome lettuce, French beans, early peppers and sweet carrots. I like to see the first carrots of summer on sale in bunches with their fresh, green leaves. I use them for many different soups, in a salad with orange and mange-tout in carrot cake, cooked with lovage, and in crisp salads with fennel.

Blackcurrants appear in our vegetable garden and inspire my cheesecake on page 97, and savoury recipes with kidneys or duck. A crown roast of lamb is stuffed with red currant mixture (see page 50), and I make many sauces with these currants to freeze for later months. It is the time for barbecues, and for chilled soups, sorbets, ice-cream, salmon, trout and home-made herb vinegars.

Cold summer soups, like cucumber, gazpacho and carrot with orange should be less substantial than hot winter soups. They are intended as appetizers rather than filling courses, and should be served, prettily garnished with herbs, in small bowls. Salads should be excellent in the summer, with the wide range of leaves and herbs available. Subtle salads made from young leaves need a delicate dressing based on sunflower oil and lemon. Only use olive oil, wine vinegar and mustard dressings for the stronger-tasting salad ingredients.

Food can look exotic at this time of the year. Serve low-fat cheese hearts on a coulis of red summer fruits (see page 91). Garnish raspberry dishes with a perfect pink rose-bud, or finish off a lemon mousse with a large yellow rose. It is edible if sugared, so brush the petals with egg-white and dust with castor sugar. Just before serving, snip away all the stem of the rose, and arrange on the pudding. In summer, the possibilities are endless.

STARTERS

Don't throw away the inch-long thinnings of beetroot, carrots and parsnips. They taste and look beautiful. The effort of digging, hoeing and weeding becomes worthwhile. They're the first fruits of love.

Carrot, orange and mange-tout salad

This beautiful-looking and tasty first course was inspired the last time we thinned our carrots and had minute vegetables available. It happily coincided with the first mange-tout of the season. But if you do not grow vegetables, you can still serve this by making a julienne of carrots and using fairly small mange-tout. Clean and prepare the vegetables first, then boil them with the rind of orange for one minute. Drain and refresh in cold water. *Photograph on page 67.*

3 oz/75 g carrots
4 or 5 oz/100 or 150 g mange-tout
1 orange, with $\frac{1}{4}$ of its rind pared and cut into needle threads
black pepper
1 tbsp lemon juice
2 tbsp chopped fresh lovage
chervil or tarragon (whole leaves to decorate)

Make the dressing and add the orange rind. Arrange the mange-tout, carrots and orange segments in a circle on individual plates. Decorate with fresh herbs and pour over dressing. Serve immediately. Nasturtium flowers and leaves are also perfect for decorating this dish because they complement the orange and green colours. But they are not always available so early in the summer.

Page 67
Carrot, orange and mange-tout salad

Baby beetroot creams

The first beetroot of the season are needed for this recipe, which we have when we thin out the row, but tiny beetroot are now sold by many shops. I serve one beetroot per person in an individual white ramekin dish, and the white sauce soon becomes pink from the beetroot. This is the most attractive time of year to serve it. It does look beautiful.

4 small beetroot	**2 tbsp spring onions or chives, chopped**
4 oz/100 g plain yoghurt	**1 spring onion to garnish**
1 tbsp lemon juice*	**black pepper**

68

(*1 tbsp of home-made horseradish sauce, using yoghurt instead of cream, can be used instead of the lemon juice to make a change.)

Wash the beetroot and cook in boiling water for about an hour. Rub off the skins when they are cooked, and put one in each small white dish. Make the sauce from the other ingredients. Pour over the beetroot. Garnish with a spring onion tassel (see page 28), or when chives are in flower, substitute chopped chives for the spring onions, and garnish with the pink chive flowers.

Avocados with a green heart

Although avocados are available throughout the year, they are most plentiful in the summer, when they can look so attractive with summer salads and subtle first courses. My first recipe is a favourite, despite not being as subtle as many other avocado dishes I serve. The different shades of green mixed together look very attractive. *Photograph on page 71.*

Salad leaves
2 avocados
1 small green pepper
8 spring onions
1 tbsp chives, chopped
1 tbsp chervil, chopped
DRESSING
6 tbsp green olive oil
2 tbsp white-wine vinegar
a pinch dry mustard
a pinch of sugar
pepper
crushed garlic

Mix the dressing ingredients together. Halve the avocados. Chop the pepper and 4 of the spring onions together, including most of the green part. Mix with the herbs and dressing. Divide into 4 and spoon into the avocado halves. Arrange on the salad leaves to make heart shapes. Garnish with spring onion tassels (see page 28) and chervil sprigs.

Spicy sorrel soup

I was reading the newspaper while having a marvellous breakfast, of smoked salmon with scrambled eggs, high above the clouds on a flight south from New York, when I was insired by a recipe in the *New York Times*. When I returned home, I made my first sorrel soup with the sorrel I was growing for the first time in my new herb garden.

The recipe had 6 eggs and 3 'cups of heavy cream', as Americans often describe double cream, so it had to be modified considerably. It was the idea of sharpening the already sharp sorrel with Indian spices that appealed to me. It is now a popular soup in my household. It is good hot or cold. *Photograph opposite.*

1½ lb/700 g sorrel
1 oz/25 g margarine
1 onion, finely chopped
1 pt/600 ml chicken stock
1–2 tbsp curry powder (depending on strength), or a mixture of garam masala, ground cumin, coriander and chilli powder
4 oz/100 g plain yoghurt
1 egg yolk
pepper

Wash the sorrel and remove the stems. Shred and cook it briefly in half the margarine. In a separate pan, soften the onion, add the spices, and then the stock. Add the sorrel, simmer for 5 minutes, and liquidize. Add the yoghurt, egg yolk and seasoning. Do not boil, or it will curdle.

Page 71
Avocado with a green heart.
Spicy sorrel soup

Iced avocado and cucumber soup

1 onion, chopped finely
1 tbsp oil
2 ripe avocados
1 cucumber chopped, with a few thin slices reserved
1½ pt/900 ml chicken stock
juice of half a lemon
pepper
dill (optional) or a little fresh herb for cooking and garnish
thick yoghurt

Soften the onion in the oil, add the stock and chunks of cucumber. Simmer for 2 or 3 minutes. Liquidize with the avocado flesh and dill. Season and heat slowly to scalding point. Chill. Sharpen with lemon juice to taste. Serve in individual bowls, with a cucumber ring, a piece of dill and a blob of yoghurt in each one.

Guacamole

2 ripe avocados
juice of 1 lemon
1 clove garlic, mashed
4 tomatoes, chopped
1 small onion, finely chopped
4 tbsp green pepper, finely chopped
1 tbsp parsley, chopped
3 tbsp oil
pepper

Peel and mash the avocados with a wooden spoon. Mix with all the other ingredients and spoon into individual serving dishes. By keeping the stones in the mixture until serving, you will prevent it from browning.

Avocado beans

Broad beans are an important reason for growing vegetables. We just cannot eat enough of them. This is an unusual way of serving them as a starter, when they can look particularly pretty with the different shades of greens. Savory is the perfect herb to serve with this vegetable; summer savory is better than winter savory for this dish, but either will do. The dish provides a good chance of enjoying the three main tastes of avocado, bean and herb. *Photograph on page 90.*

2 avocados
8 oz/225 g shelled broad beans
2 tsp chopped savory
pepper
juice of one lemon
2 oz/50 g plain yoghurt
1 tbsp olive oil

Cook the beans, then cool and skin them. Slice the avocados and sprinkle them with lemon juice. Mix together the yoghurt, oil and pepper. Arrange the vegetables artistically on 4 individual plates, pour over the yoghurt sauce and sprinkle on the chopped savory.

Avocado oranges

2 avocados
1 orange
1 pink grapefruit
½ lemon
lemon slices for garnish
FRENCH DRESSING
3 tbsp green olive oil
1 tbsp lemon juice
pepper
chervil or parsley, chopped

Peel the avocados, orange and grapefruit and cut into thin slices. Arrange alternatively in a circle on the plate, with a sprig of chervil in the centre. Make a dressing from the oil, chervil, lemon juice and pepper, and sprinkle over. Garnish with lemon slices.

Carrot soup

This soup is at its best with a good home-made chicken stock and fresh home-grown carrots. It has an exquisitely delicate flavour. But it is also excellent, even if you have to resort to a stock cube and ancient carrots.

1 lb/450 g carrots, scrubbed and sliced
1 onion, chopped
2 leeks, chopped
2 pt/1.1 l chicken stock
fresh chives, or lovage if available
6 oz/175 g plain yoghurt
1 tbsp oil
pepper

Soften the onion and leeks in the hot oil, then add the carrots for several minutes. Add the stock. Simmer until the carrots are cooked, and then liquidize. Mix in the yoghurt and serve garnished with chopped herbs.

Summer seafood salad

This salad looks beautiful and tastes cool on a summer's day, with its pretty combination of pink fish and green herbs. Choose the fish for their colour and firm texture, including prawns, scallops, mussels, pink squid, and even salmon or lobster if you feel grand. *Photograph opposite.*

2 lb/900 g of mixed seafood
DRESSING
juice of 2 lemons
6 tbsp green olive oil
1 bunch of spring onions, half finely chopped
2 cupfuls of fresh herbs, sticking to subtle flavours like
    parsley, tarragon, chervil, dill or chives
1 lb/450 g brown rice
pepper

*Page 75
Summer seafood salad*

Cook and cool the rice. Poach the seafood for a very short time. The squid will need more cooking than the rest. Scallops, for example, only need about 30 seconds. Slice the scallops, take the cooked mussels out of their shells, slice the squid, and cube any large pieces of fish. Make the dressing, and mix with the herbs, chopped onions and rice. Arrange the seafood in the rice salad, and garnish with spring onion tassels (see page 28) and lemon twists. Chill for up to an hour before serving.

Courgette flan

This is a subtle, pretty, yellow and green dish to serve on a sunny summer or early autumn day. It is particularly good made with the *fromage blanc* pastry described on page 19.

6 oz /175 g green courgettes and 6 oz/175 g yellow
½ oz/15 g margarine
1 small onion, chopped
1 sprig rosemary
2 eggs
4 tbsp grated Parmesan cheese
¼ pt/150 ml thick yoghurt
dash of lemon juice
pastry to line a 9 in/23 cm flan case, baked blind
3–4 tbsp water
pepper

Cube the washed, but unpeeled courgettes and cook them with the margarine, onion, herb, lemon juice and seasoning in the water for only 1 or 2 minutes. The courgettes should still be crisp. Leave to cool. Remove the rosemary and arrange the two-coloured courgette mixture prettily in the flan case. Beat the eggs with the yoghurt and Parmesan, adjust the seasoning and pour over the courgettes. Bake in a medium oven for half an hour at least. Check it so that the top does not brown. It has most flavour served just warm, and it is most pretty when it still looks pale, yellow and green. So take care not to overcook this lovely dish, which can be served as a first course (my preference) or with salads as the central dish in a light meal.

Squash with sorrel stuffing

This is an extremely elegant start to a meal when it is made with the bright-green squash, with scalloped edges, which is just a little bigger than a tennis ball. This really is the most exotic sphere to be found in vegetable shops.

4 small green squash
4 oz/100 g cooked brown rice
1 onion, chopped
1 clove garlic
2 oz/50 g cooked lean ham, chopped

1 large handful sorrel, chopped
1 tbsp tarragon, chopped
1 tbsp lemon balm, chopped
1 tbsp oil
pepper
basil or marjoram
spicy tomato sauce (see page 46)

Wash the squash, cut off their lids and scoop out the flesh. Reserve this to steam for another meal. Soften the onion and garlic in the oil. Add the rice, pepper, ham and herbs. Mix well together and use to stuff the 4 squash. Lay them on foil, pour over the tomato sauce, cover with foil, and cook in a medium oven until the squash are soft. This should take 30 to 45 minutes. When they are ready, serve on individual plates, with a pool of the tomato sauce underneath, garnished with fresh basil or marjoram.

Raw fish salad

The perfect time for fresh Scotch Salmon is from May to July.

8 oz/225 g of raw fish, preferably salmon
1 lime
2 tsp fresh dill (or fennel if dill is not available)
1 tsp sugar
mixed salad leaves and sprouting seeds
pepper
French dressing (see page 73)

Pare 4 strips from the lime. Blanch for 2 minutes. Marinate the fish overnight in a mixture of dill, pepper, sugar, 2 of the chopped strips of lime peel and lime juice. The next day, prepare the mixed salad leaves and a French dressing from green olive oil and lime juice. Wash the raw fish and cut into 12 thin slices. Arrange 4 slices per person on a plate of salad leaves, and garnish with tomato roses (see page 29), spring onion tassels (see page 28) and lime twists (see page 30). Pour over the dressing, add a sprig of dill and serve.

Smoked salmon with smoked fish mousse

One of my friends, who relaxes from his profession as a violinist by fishing, smokes his own trout, and often gives one to me: a much-appreciated present. Smoked trout is excellent on its own, with salad, horseradish and yoghurt sauce, and edible, orange flowers, like pot marigold, or nasturtium, scattered on top. Or for an even more special meal, it can be made into a mousse to serve with smoked salmon.

1 small smoked trout	coriander, chervil or dill
8 oz/225 g smoked salmon	2 tsp grated horseradish
4 oz/100 g plain, thick yoghurt	black and cayenne pepper
1 lemon	

First, purée the flesh of the trout with the yoghurt. Add 1 tsp of finely grated, blanched lemon rind, and at least 2 tsp of grated horseradish. Add the lemon juice, cayenne and black pepper to taste, or even more horseradish if you like it hot. Arrange the smoke salmon on salad leaves, garnish with lemon or lime, and serve with the trout mousse and wholemeal bread.

Salmon mousse with watercress sauce

8 oz/225 g fresh salmon
1 egg
$\frac{1}{2}$ oz/15 g margarine
8 oz/225 g *fromage frais*
pepper
WATERCRESS SAUCE
6 oz/175 g watercress
1 oz/25 g margarine
4 oz/100 g *fromage frais*
$\frac{1}{2}$ tsp white-wine vinegar

Page 79
Smoked salmon with smoked fish mousse

Blend the salmon mousse ingredients together. Put into 4 greased ramekins, and bake in a bain-marie in a hot oven for 15 to 20 minutes. Make the sauce by pulling off the watercress leaves, heat them through in the margarine, and then add to wine vinegar and *fromage frais*. Heat gently and put a pool of the sauce on 4 plates. Then turn out the salmon mousse, garnish with chives, blobs of *fromage frais* and watercress leaves.

Herb soufflés

Individual herb soufflés make an unusual and refreshing first course. They can be subtle, made with the classic combination of chervil, tarragon and parsley, or slightly bitter with the celery-flavoured herb, lovage. I like lovage soufflé, but find that it is at its best when the lovage leaves are young and fresh. By late summer and autumn, the leaves taste too strong for this recipe.

a handful of lovage leaves, or a mixture of chervil, tarragon and parsley
1 oz/25 g margarine
1 oz/25 g flour
½ pt/300 ml skimmed milk
6 eggs, separated
3 tbsp grated Parmesan cheese
1 tbsp breadcrumbs
pepper

Soften the herbs in the melted margarine. Add the flour and then stir in the milk gradually. Purée, cool, and add the 6 egg yolks. Add half the Parmesan and the pepper. Grease 4 ramekins, and then stir in the whipped egg-whites into the herb mixture. Fill the ramekins, and put the breadcrumbs and remainder of the cheese on top. Cook in a hot oven for about 10 minutes, till the soufflés have risen, but are still a little moist in the middle.

Summer smoked mackerel pâté

2 small mackerel fillets
4 tbsp plain yoghurt
½ tbsp lemon thyme
2 tbsp lemon juice
paprika and black pepper to taste

Take the flesh off the mackerel fillets and liquidize with the other ingredients. Leave to set in the refrigerator. This can be transformed into a more special dish by rolling the pâté in smoked salmon, and serving slices on mixed salad leaves, dressed, and garnished with lemon and sprigs of lemon thyme.

Ginger prawns

This recipe, which satisfies my love of sesame oil and ginger, can be served as a light main course, or as a first course on individual plates, serving two large prawns per person.

8 giant prawns
2 tbsp sesame oil
1 in/2.5 cm root ginger
1 large clove garlic
2 tsp lemon juice
pepper
nice salad ingredients like nasturtium leaves or flowers
crisp lettuce, endive and radicchio

Wash the salad, dry, and make a dressing from 1 tbsp of the oil, the lemon juice, a little garlic, and the pepper. Toss the salad in the dressing. Heat through the prawns in warm sesame oil in which the finely chopped garlic and ginger have been cooked. After about 2 minutes, serve the warm prawns and their tasty juices of ginger on top of the salad.

Herrings on a bed of sorrel

Summer is a good time to eat this healthy dish, because shoals of herrings appear around our island when gardens and markets are offering sorrel at its freshest. The first, baby leaves of sorrel appear in spring.

4 fat herrings
2 tbsp oil
4 tbsp breadcrumbs
8 oz/225 g sorrel, chopped
3 tbsp *fromage blanc*
pepper
juice of a lemon

Clean and season the fish, and colour them on both sides in hot oil. Put them in an ovenproof dish, add the lemon juice and breadcrumbs and bake in medium oven for 10 to 15 minutes. Remove and add the sorrel around the fish, bake for another 10 minutes. Then add *fromage blanc* and serve with potatoes in their skins.

MAIN COURSES

Spicy stuffed peppers

Peppers are now grown commercially by a neighbour of mine in no less than five colours – green, red, yellow, white and purplish-black – so beautiful dishes of multi-coloured raw peppers can now be assembled.

But, unfortunately, raw peppers give me, and many other people, indigestion, so I prefer to eat them cooked in some way. I was disappointed, however, when I first cooked the new black peppers, to discover that they do lose their lovely colour. Try serving a spicy tomato soup in the raw, prepared peppers (cut in half), and then saving them for the next day to stuff in the following way. This is not only a very pretty dish, with its multi-coloured peppers, but it tastes so much more refreshing than the normal bland vegetable stuffing.

8 peppers
8 oz/225 g minced lamb fillet
1 onion, chopped
2 tbsp oil
1–1$\frac{1}{2}$ cup rice
1 clove garlic
1 tsp turmeric
3 tsp garam masala
1$\frac{1}{2}$ tsp powdered cumin
$\frac{1}{4}$ tsp chilli powder
pepper
fresh coriander

Remove the tops and pips from the peppers and cook them in boiling water for 4 minutes. Cook the rice in the water for 30 minutes. Drain and leave to cool. Cook the onion and garlic in oil for 3 minutes, add the minced lamb for another 5 minutes, and then add all the spices. When they are blended in, mix well with the rice, add 2 tablespoons of chopped coriander and use this to stuff the peppers. Bake, covered, in a medium oven for 30 minutes. Serve hot, with a yoghurt sauce, or cold on a bed of salad, with fresh lemon to squeeze on top. Garnish in either case with fresh coriander.

Squid speciale

I love squid in almost any form – in a mixed seafood salad, stuffed with nuts and brown rice, or in this colourful recipe which can be eaten with brown bread as a tasty, robust first course, or with salad and rice as a main meal.

$1\frac{1}{2}$ lb/700 g squid, chopped
3 shallots, chopped
2 cloves garlic
2 tbsp marjoram, chopped
1 tbsp oil
4 tomatoes, chopped
1 glass red wine
juice of half a lemon
about 12 fat black olives
pepper

Soften the chopped shallots and garlic in oil for a few minutes, and then add the chopped squid, herb and pepper. Cook for a little longer, then add all the other ingredients and simmer until the squid is opaque and tender. This should be served garnished with marjoram. Golden marjoram looks particularly attractive with the black and red colours of this recipe. Parsley, coriander or chervil can also be used if fresh marjoram is not available when you want to cook this dish.

Sesame fish grill

4 fillets of fish, like sole or plaice
3 tbsp sesame oil
1 tbsp soy sauce
1 clove garlic, finely chopped
4 spring onions, finely chopped
1 in/2.5 cm root ginger, finely chopped
2 tbsp sesame seeds
pepper
4 spring onion tassels (see page 28) to garnish

Wash the fish, dry, and then smear their surface with a mixture of the sesame oil and soy sauce. Mix the garlic, spring onions and root ginger with the sesame seeds, sprinkle over the fish, add the pepper, and grill as normal.

Baked fish with a dill and cucumber sauce

This recipe is suitable for any large fish that is to be baked whole, like sea bass or even salmon trout.

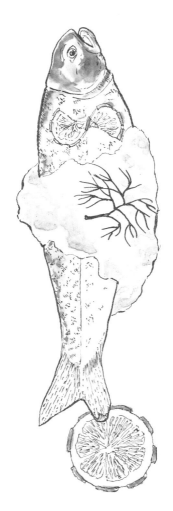

1 large fish of 3 to 4 lb/1.5 to 2 kg
1 lemon
pepper
½ cucumber, finely chopped
4 tbsp fish stock
2 tbsp *fromage blanc*
dill
oil

Put the shell of half a lemon and a sprig of dill inside the prepared fish. Rub the fish with oil, add pepper, and sprinkle with half the lemon juice. Wrap loosely in foil and bake in a medium oven until tender, probably 45 minutes to an hour. Serve with a sauce cooked by simmering the finely chopped cucumber in the fish stock and juice of half a lemon, season, and after just 1 minute's cooking, stir in the *fromage blanc*. Add a little blanched lemon rind and chopped dill just before serving. Garnish the whole fish with lemon and sprigs of dill.

Tangy tarragon chicken

1 plump chicken of 3 or 4 lb/1.5 to 2 kg
2 tbsp tarragon mustard
1 tbsp honey
finely chopped rind of half an orange
juice from the whole orange
¼ pt/150 ml chicken stock
2 tbsp sherry
fresh tarragon
pepper

Mix the mustard with the honey and spread all over the roasting chicken. Roast in a medium oven for 1 to 1½ hours, with half the orange shell and the fresh tarragon in the cavity, basting with the juices forming in the stock and orange juice. When cooked, keep the chicken warm, remove fats from the cooking juices, and then add the sherry and reduce to a good consistency. Garnish with orange and fresh tarragon.

Chicken and walnuts

4 chicken breasts
1 tbsp walnut oil
4 oz/100 g walnuts, chopped and pounded
⅓ pt/200 ml chicken stock
1 glass of white wine
3 tbsp *fromage blanc*
pepper

Cook the chicken breasts in the walnut oil for 3 minutes on each side. Put in the oven to keep warm. Add the walnuts to the pan with the wine and stock, and simmer until the sauce is of a thick consistency. Add the *fromage blanc*. Pour over the breasts and serve with potatoes in skins and a green salad or vegetable.

Lemon chicken

I find a terracotta chicken brick very useful for slow, low-fat cooking and I use it for both the following family favourites.

1 large roasting chicken
herbs (1 bay-leaf, piece of lemon thyme, parsley stalk)
2 large lemons
1 glass white wine
3 tbsp *fromage blanc*
pepper
chicken stock

Wash a good fat chicken, put the herbs inside, with the lemon skins. Pepper well, put in the chicken brick with the wine and cook slowly for at least 2 hours in a medium oven. Take out and keep the chicken warm. Pour the fat off the juices and put in a pan with a little concentrated chicken stock, the juice of the 2 lemons, and heat through, thickening with the *fromage blanc*. Serve with baked potatoes and a green vegetable.

Tarragon chicken in a brick

1 large roasting chicken,
3 sprigs of fresh tarragon
pepper
1 glass cooking brandy
4 tbsp *fromage blanc*

Cook the chicken in a brick, as above, but brown and then flame it with the brandy first. Use 2 of the tarragon sprigs inside the chicken. When it is cooked, remove the fat from the sauce, which will by now be well-flavoured with the brandy and tarragon, and thicken with the *fromage blanc*. Serve the chicken coated in the sauce, with fresh chopped tarragon scattered on top. Excellent with new potatoes in their skins and a crisp green salad.

Kidneys with blackcurrant sauce

12 lambs' kidneys
8 oz/225 g fresh blackcurrants, plus 2 or 3 small bunches with leaves for garnish
1 tbsp black currant jam
2 tbsp *Crème de Cassis*
1½ oz/40 g margarine
1 oz/25 g sugar
3 tbsp red-wine vinegar
¼ pt/150 ml good beef stock
pepper
2 tbsp water

Prepare and slice the kidneys. Pepper well and cook them for about 5 minutes in the margarine, turning so that they brown evenly. Transfer them to a warm oven, reserving the juices. Cook the blackcurrants for 3 to 4 minutes in no more than 2 tablespoons of water in a separate pan. Add the jam to the kidney juices, with the wine vinegar, and reduce until it is thick and syrupy. Then add the *Cassis*, stock, sugar and black currants. Check the seasoning, and cook for about 10 minutes until the sauce is a suitable consistency for coating the kidneys. Serve with a plain green vegetable, like broccoli, garnishing the dish with fresh bunches of black currants and their leaves.

A delicious syrup for sorbets can be made by infusing young black currant leaves in the liquid. The leaves can then be used for garnishing the kidney dish, if you wish.

Page 87
Kidneys with blackcurrant
sauce

Chicken with grapes

1 fresh roasting chicken
1 lb /450 g seedless grapes, halved
⅓ pt/200 ml chicken stock
1 glass dry white wine
pepper
3 tbsp *fromage blanc*
tarragon

Roast the chicken in the normal way, well seasoned and with a sprig of a fresh herb like tarragon inside. Cut each grape in half. Add the chicken stock and wine to the fat-free juices from the roasting pan. Add the grapes and simmer for 5 minutes till the sauce is thickening slightly. Add the pepper and *fromage blanc*. Heat through, and serve poured over the chicken. Garnish with small bunches of grapes, and sprigs of tarragon.

VEGETABLES

Almond asparagus

One of the great delights of the last two or three years is that because asparagus can now be bought so cheaply, we eat it regularly when it is in season. It must, of course, be very fresh. I prefer it cooked and served very simply, with lemon juice or a French dressing. Asparagus has to be cooked carefully because of its combination of a woody stem and tender tip, so I cut off the base end and reserve for soups and sauces, and then steam the green tips for no more than 10 minutes. The exact time depends on its thickness. If asparagus is cooked in the same pan as new potatoes, they take on its delicious flavour.

2 lb/900 g asparagus
2 oz/50 g toasted split almonds
3 tbsp thick plain yoghurt
juice of half a lemon
pepper

Steam the asparagus tips for 10 minutes. Then put in a shallow dish, and pour over a sauce made by heating the other ingredients together very gently.

New potatoes dressed for dinner with caviare

This is a very special way of serving potatoes to celebrate the first of the season. But they are also marvellous on their own early in the summer, especially if they are cooked and eaten immediately after being lifted from the ground. The taste of the newest of the new potatoes makes me understand a friend's euphoria many years ago after eating a meal, consisting just of potatoes. He was on holiday in Ireland and a local farmer asked him to join the family at dinner. Dinner was potatoes and as the guest, my friend was given the pick of the new crop. He said potatoes had never tasted finer. *Photograph on page 90.*

16 small new potatoes
4 tbsp olive oil
pepper
5 spring onions, chopped
3 tbsp *fromage blanc*
1 tbsp tarragon vinegar
4 tbsp black caviare
tarragon leaves
lemon slices and spring onion tassels
   (see page 28) to garnish

Wash the potatoes, but as normal do not peel. Toss in half the oil and pepper, and bake in a hot oven for about 40 minutes until they are tender. When cool, cut in half, scoop out the flesh and mash it in a bowl. Add to it the *fromage blanc*, chopped spring onions and rest of the pepper. Put back into the skins and chill. Make a dressing with the rest of the oil and the tarragon vinegar, spoon over the potato halves, and then decorate with caviare on top. Garnish with lemon twists, tarragon and spring onion tassels.

PUDDINGS

COULIS OF SUMMER FRUITS

I find that the soft, red fruits of the summer are a special treat year after year. I never tire of their perfect looks and their fresh, fresh tastes. And I never fail to find new ways of making the most of their attributes every June, July, August and September.

One special thing to do with any of these red fruits which are not in perfect shape is to make a smooth sauce, or coulis, of their combined flavours. It can be stored in the fridge to use for puddings and cocktails: 2 tablespoons of the following coulis in a glass of champagne makes a perfect cocktail and 4 oz/100 g of coulis per person is about right as the base of the pudding.

Coulis recipe

1 lb/450 g red, soft fruits, like strawberries, raspberries and red currants
8 oz/225 g sorbet syrup (see below)
juice of 1 lemon

Prepare and wash the fruit and make into a purée with the syrup and lemon juice. Pass it through a fine sieve. This will keep for several days in the fridge

Sorbet syrup

2 lb/900 g sugar
2½ pt/1.5 l water
6 oz/175 g glucose

Put all 3 ingredients into a thick pan and boil for about 10 minutes. Skim the surface when necessary, and then pass through a fine sieve and leave to cool. I like to use herbs, including sweet cicely or the leaves of the black currant, to flavour the syrup, as I describe on page 86. A syrup of this kind will keep for 2 weeks in the fridge, and it will also freeze, of course.

Page 90
New potatoes dressed for
dinner with caviare.
Avocado beans

Raspberry ice-cream

Raspberries make one of the very best yoghurt-based ice-creams. The flavours of the fresh fruit and plain yoghurt mix well.

1 lb/450 g raspberries, reserving half of the best-looking fruit to use whole
2 oz/50 g sugar
1 lb/450 g plain yoghurt
3 oz/75 g wild blossom honey

Purée half the fruit with the sugar and honey. Sieve the purée to give a smooth final product. Add the yoghurt and then proceed to make the ice-cream by either of the methods described on page 64. Serve 1 large circle of ice-cream surrounded by fresh uncooked raspberries, 4 oz/100 g of coulis as the base, and garnished with crystallized mint leaves (see page 27).

Raspberry and melon surprise

1 lb/450 g raspberry ice-cream (see above)
1 large honeydew melon
2 tbsp lemon juice
1 tsp mint, chopped
sprigs of crystallized mint

Chop the melon flesh and liquidize it with the lemon juice and chopped mint. Chill. Pour this into pretty, shallow bowls, and put a scoop of raspberry ice-cream into the centre of each. Garnish with crystallized mint, whole raspberries and melon balls. Instead of ice-cream, raspberries can be heated through in liquor and added to the centre of the iced melon soup.

Raspberry snow

1 tbsp brandy
10 oz/275 g raspberries
3 mint leaves for garnish

Make the yoghurt snow as described on page 65. Add the brandy, and fold in the raspberries. Spoon into individual glasses, chill, and serve garnished with 1 raspberry and the mint leaves.

Charantais melon with Dubonnet raspberries

2 chilled melons, halved
1 lb/450 g raspberries
4 tbsp Dubonnet
2 tbsp syrup, flavoured by infusing with the herb sweet cicely, if available

Put the raspberries in a mixture of the syrup and Dubonnet and leave for a few hours to soak up the flavour. Halve the melons, remove the seeds, and slice a little from the base so they stand firmly on each individual serving plate. Spoon the raspberries into the melons, garnish with sweet cicely, and serve while still chilled.

FRUIT WINE JELLY

This is an extremely beautiful pudding, which allows the artist to show off at the end of a meal. Choose glamorous red fruits which will look at their best in the red-wine jelly. When I served this, wobbling on a large, oval, Victorian, white fluted dish, the friends sitting around the table shrieked with surprise. They thought the fruit juices would fall in their laps. The fact that a jelly was holding all the fruit in place was kept a secret until the pudding was safely in place on the table.

Jelly recipe

1 orange
1 tsp powdered gelatine
$\frac{1}{4}$ pt/150 ml red wine
1 tbsp orange flower water (if unavailable vanilla essence can be used instead)
a pinch of powdered cinnamon

FRUIT RECIPES

Any combination can be used. I chose the following:

1 pink grapefruit
1 blood orange
12 strawberries
8 raspberries (or use loganberries if you can)
6 cherries
about 20 red currants
a handful of sweet cicely or mint leaves

To make the jelly, grate the rind and squeeze the juice of the orange. Soak the rind in the juice, while softening the gelatine in the wine. After it has softened, heat it in the wine to dissolve. Add the cinnamon, strained orange juice and then the orange water. Cool it till it begins to set, and then pour on to 1 large, chilled serving plate, or 4 individual chilled plates. Segment the orange and grapefruit, halve the strawberries and cherries, and prepare the smaller red fruit. When the jelly has almost set, arrange the fruit artistically with a whole raspberry, loganberry or strawberry in the centre. Serve, scattered with finely shredded mint, or preferably the prettier sweet cicely if you have some available.

INDIVIDUAL WINE JELLIES

Small moulds or Alcan icebags can be used to make pretty, assorted fruit and wine jellies to serve with mixed fresh fruit. Many combinations are possible, but try the wine jelly recipe above divided into 8 to 10 small moulds, served with mango slices, mango jelly, fresh strawberries, sliced kumquats and kiwi fruit jelly. This makes a beautiful plateful of red, green and orange colours which can be garnished with mint or sweet cicely. *Photograph opposite.*

Mango Jelly

1 ripe mango
$\frac{1}{4}$ pt/150 ml fresh orange juice
1 sachet of gelatine

Soak the gelatine in the orange juice, then dissolve over gentle heat. Add it to the puréed and sieved mango. Pour into small, pretty jelly moulds.

Kiwi fruit jelly

8 kiwi fruit
juice of 2 limes
1 sachet of geltine

Purée and sieve the fruit. Extract the lime juice, and make the jelly as described in the recipe above.

Page 95
Wine jelly

WILD FLOWER PUDDINGS

Wild flowers, like violet and primrose, can be used in spring salads, and crystallized for puddings, but perhaps there is nothing more useful than the two flowers of summer – elderflower and meadowsweet. Elderflowers make wonderful wine, but they also make the sorbet on page 101, and impart very special flavour to gooseberry fool. Until recently I knew less about the joys of meadowsweet. Because of our damp climate, it thrives all over Britain, and I first began picking it to dry for pot-pourri. But then I tried stewing it with summer fruits, like gooseberries, and found that it sweetens puddings rather like honey.

Meadowsweet apricots

4 flower heads of meadowsweet for the pudding, and more for garnish
1 lb/450 g apricots
⅓ pt/200 ml white wine
2 oz/50 g slivered almonds

Halve and stone the apricots and simmer for 10 minutes with the flowers and wine. Remove the flower heads, sprinkle with the almonds, and serve hot with yoghurt snow flavoured with brandy (see page 65). Serve in a pretty bowl, standing on a larger plate, so that meadowsweet can be strewn around the pudding to provide a talking point.

Cherry strudel

½ lb/200 g filo pastry
3 lb/1.5 kg morello cherries
4 oz/100 g ground almonds
3 oz/75 g breadcrumbs
4 oz/100 g sugar
1 tsp ground cinnamon
oil for brushing pastry

Stone the cherries and wash well. Mix all the ingredients together. Lay out the pastry sheets on a large surface, overlapping each piece. Put the mixture evenly over half the pastry nearest to you. Turn over the pastry in a roll. Brush with oil and cook on a greased baking-tray in a hot oven for about 20 minutes. When brown, remove from the oven, and dust with a little icing sugar, if you wish.

Blackcurrant cheesecake

This dish looks superb on a dish with a central pedestal, like a white, ceramic cake-stand, or a Victorian dish in this style. I serve mine on a blue-and-white Victorian cake-dish, which looks beautiful with the blues and purples of the blackcurrants and borage. *Photograph on page 155.*

2 oz/50 g melted margarine
4 oz/100 g digestive biscuits, crushed
1 oz/25 g muscovado sugar
1 oz/25 g castor sugar
2 eggs, separated
grated rind and juice of 1 lemon
$\frac{1}{2}$ oz/15 g gelatine
1 lb/450 g thick *fromage blanc* (like Quark)
BLACKCURRANT TOPPING
8 oz/225 g fresh black currants
2 tbsp *Crème de Cassis*
1 tsp arrowroot
1 small bunch fresh blackcurrants
borage flowers (if available)

Combine the biscuits, dark sugar and margarine. Then spread over the base of an oiled 7- or 8-inch/18- or 20-cm loose-bottomed cake tin. Put in the fridge until firm.

Beat the egg yolks, white sugar and half the lemon rind into the *fromage blanc*. Soak the gelatine in the lemon juice, and then heat until dissolved. Stir into the cheese mixture. Whisk the egg-whites till stiff and fold into the mixture. Spread over the tin's base and keep in the fridge until firm.

Gently heat the blackcurrants in a pan with the *Crème de Cassis*, until soft and syrupy. Thicken the mixture with arrowroot, if necessary. When cool, put it on top of the cheesecake, and decorate with a small bunch of fresh blackcurrants and 2 or 3 leaves, a little of the lemon rind, and some of the delicate blue flowers of borage if they are available.

Summer pudding

8–10 slices of thin wholemeal bread with crusts removed
6 oz/175 g raspberries
6 oz/175 g blackcurrants
4 oz/100 g strawberries
juice of half a lemon
a little water
BLACKCURRANT SAUCE
1 oz/25 g blackcurrants
1 or more tbsp sugar
FOR GARNISH
some icing sugar
borage flowers if available
3 strawberries
3 raspberries
2 bunches of black currants
young black currant leaves or mint

Line a 1½ pt/900 ml bowl with bread. Stew the fruit gently, adding lemon juice, a little water and, if necessary, a little sugar. Pour into the bowl, top with bread, cover that with some of the fruit's juice, and leave to cool overnight. Make the sauce. Turn out the pudding and serve with garnish. *Photograph opposite.*

Strawberry sugar glaze

8 oz/225 g strawberries, halved
2 tbsp liqueur of choice (Cassis, Grand Marnier or Kirsch, for example)
6 oz/175 g plain Greek-style yoghurt
4 oz/100 g sugar

Put the strawberries in liqueur into 4 individual ramekins. Pour over the yoghurt. Chill for about an hour. Sprinkle the sugar over the surface and put under a hot grill briefly, until the sugar caramelizes.

*Page 99
Summer pudding*

Rose petal ice-cream

4 pink, scented roses
½ oz/15 g gelatine
1 tbsp rose water
1 tsp lemon juice
2 oz/50 g flaked almonds, toasted
8 oz/225 g plain thick yoghurt
6 oz/175 g honey
½ pt/300 ml water
crystallized rose petals for garnish (see page 27)

Dissolve the honey in the water. Simmer the rose petals in this for 10 minutes. Add the dissolved gelatine, lemon juice and rose water, and then cool. When the mixture is half-set, fold in the thick yoghurt and half the almonds. Leave to set completely, and serve garnished with the almonds and crystallized rose petals.

Kirsch summer fruit salad

1 very large pineapple
4 oz/100 g black grapes, skinned and pipped
8 oz/225 g fresh lychees, peeled
4 oz/100 g raspberries
4 oz/100 g strawberries (if they are large, they should be halved)
juice of half a lemon
6 tbsp Kirsch
½ tbsp lemon balm, chopped
lemon balm for garnish

Cut the pineapple into half lengthways, and carefully scoop out the flesh. Cube the pineapple flesh. Add it to all the other fruit in a bowl, and toss in the lemon juice, lemon balm and Kirsch. Leave to soak up the flavours for about 2 hours in the fridge, then pile the fruit back into the pineapple halves, and garnish with lemon balm.

Elderflower sorbet

½ pt/300 ml water
¼ pt/150 ml dry white wine
4 oz/100 g castor sugar
2 oz/50 g elderflower heads
1 egg-white
juice of 2 lemons, finely grated rind of 1

Heat together the water, wine, sugar and lemon rind. Boil, and then simmer for several minutes. Add the elderflowers and lemon juice and leave to cool. Strain, and use to make the sorbet with the whisked egg-white in the normal way. Serve in scoops, decorated with elderflowers.

AUTUMN

Autumn is the time for laying down reserves for the winter, just like a squirrel. These are the months for bottling fruit, making jam, and looking for interesting and often ancient recipes for preserves, like my spiced quince and crab-apples on pages 140 and 141. It is the time to combine crisp walks in the countryside with collecting interesting ingredients for wine, preserves, soups and even more.

In the autumn, mixed with the glowing hips, haws and beautiful berries, as well as the leaves of coppery colours, there is still food to be had for free. There are sweet chestnuts, late blackberries, crab-apples, quinces and sloes.

The interesting black sloes are found on blackthorn bushes. Last autumn I found really juicy sloes, as big as damsons. Although they are mainly a country find, they do exist in towns – even *en masse* in west London. They have an acrid taste, but they are useful for many recipes apart from the traditional sloe gin or sloe vodka. This year I have produced sloe wine and sloe chutney (made with raisins and brown sugar). Sloe and apple jelly is another treat. Make it as for other jellies – using half sloe and half apple.

I also spend a lot of time picking elderberries and blackberries. The former make syrup, sorbets and jelly. The latter are used in autumn pudding and as a sauce with venison.

Sweet chestnuts can also be found in both the town and country. I have collected pounds in less than half an hour in Richmond Park – filling our woolly hats with them and then taking them home to make chestnut soup. And if you can find quinces, make quince marmalade (Mrs Beaton's famous book contains the best recipe) or try delicious quince jam, and my quince ice-cream on page 138.

This is the season of gluts, when friends with apple, pear, quince and plum trees become very generous. Storing fruits in the attic never really works. They taste much better when they are fresh, so in the autumn I make lots of food with these fruits, and the rest I give away.

There is also often a glut of tomatoes and cucumbers, as people clear out their greenhouses. I buy trays of imperfect tomatoes from a local grower, and make pints of sauce for the freezer. Corn on the cob makes a welcome return; peppers and aubergines are at their best; artichokes are available; and interesting autumnal vegetables appear on every menu.

The fish choices of the season are skate and scallops. And then there is game. Hare, rabbits, pheasant, pigeon, wild duck and venison: we enjoy them all.

AVAILABILITY OF GAME

Grouse: late August to late October.
Guinea-fowl: throughout the year, but they are at their best in the spring.
Hare: September to March.
Mallard: September to late January.
Partridge: September to late January.
Pheasant: October to late January.
Pigeon: all year, but they are best from August to October.
Venison: June to January.

STARTERS

Apple and fennel soup

Apples are one of the delights of autumn, because then they are fresh sharp 'real' apples! I don't use apples so much during the other three seasons, because I am tired of those dull-tasting and bright-green-coloured spheres that are sold under the name of 'apples', but are not anything like the genuine article. I am also not too keen on cooking apples, and prefer to cook with the more scented and subtle English eating apples, like the Cox's and similar varieties, which are green with just a touch of red or russet.

3 sharp eating apples, sliced
1 medium-sized bulb of fennel, sliced
2 shallots, sliced
1 pt/600 ml vegetable or chicken stock
4 tbsp plain yoghurt, preferably the thick Greek type
1 tbsp chives, chopped
pepper

Cook the shallots, fennel and peeled apples in half the stock till they are soft. Cool, and blend with the rest of the stock, half the yoghurt, pepper and chives. Chill, and serve in individual bowls garnished with the rest of the yoghurt, chive flowers and fronds of fennel.

Bortsch

1 clove garlic, chopped
1 large onion, chopped
1 tbsp oil
1½ pt/900 ml chicken stock
2 cooked beetroots
4 oz/100 g thick Greek-style yoghurt
pepper
dill

Soften the chopped garlic and onion in the oil. Grate the beetroot and add with the stock and seasoning. Simmer gently until coloured and well-flavoured with beetroot. Be careful not to overcook. Liquidize and sieve, then serve with a swirl of yoghurt in each bowl and a little chopped dill.

Sweet chestnut soup

1 lb/450 g chestnuts, peeled
1 onion, chopped
2 sticks celery, chopped
1½ pt/900 ml chicken stock
1 tbsp oil
1 rasher lean bacon
croûtons (see page 31)
parsley, chopped

Grill the bacon, and then prepare the *croûtons*. Keep on one side. Then soften the chopped onion and celery in the oil, add the chestnuts and stock. Simmer for 20 minutes, purée, season and serve with the *croûtons*, parsley and crisp bacon as garnish.

Courgette and dill soup

1 onion, finely chopped
2 tbsp oil
4 medium courgettes, peeled and diced
2 pt/1 l good chicken stock
2 tbsp thick Greek yoghurt
2 tbsp chopped dill
4 dill leaves to garnish
pepper

Soften the onion in the oil for 5 minutes, add the courgettes for another 4 minutes, when they should be soft. Add the stock and simmer until completely tender. This should not take long. Purée, and warm through with yoghurt and chopped dill. Serve garnished with pieces of dill.

Cucumber soup

1 large cucumber
1 pt/600 ml chicken stock
2 tbsp plain yoghurt
mint, chopped
pepper

Wash the cucumber, but do not peel. Slice and simmer it in the stock for 5 minutes. Then liquidize, and add the yoghurt and mint. Serve cold.

Wild mushroom soup

If you go down to the woods today your big surprise is that you are far more likely to find fungi hunters than you would have done a few years ago. But whether you will find fungi to eat, will depend on your own courage and knowledge. It is very easy to go wrong and confuse one of the twenty or more edible British mushrooms with the deadly kind, so it is best to do as I do.

Inspired by a knowledgeable colleague I went into Savernake Forest in Wiltshire, an oak and beech forest in which the most delicious fungi were supposed to grow. I picked some I thought were edible, but later panicked and threw them into the bin. Perhaps I'd missed a feast. But now what I do is arm myself with a good book, like *Mushrooms* by Roger Phillips (Pan), and only go hunting with a fungi expert at my side.

1 large fresh cep or 8 oz/225 g dried ceps soaked for 1 hour in water
2 shallots, finely chopped
1 clove garlic, finely chopped
1 pt/600 ml chicken stock
1 tbsp oil
2 tbsp *fromage frais*
a little chervil if available
pepper

Soften the shallots, garlic, and then the chopped ceps. Cook for several minutes, then add the stock and pepper. Cook for 5 minutes. Then purée, and warm through with *fromage frais* and chervil.

Minted mushrooms

1 lb/450 g mushrooms, sliced
4 shallots, chopped finely
3 tbsp mint, chopped
2 cloves garlic, crushed
2 tbsp sherry vinegar
6 tbsp olive oil
pepper
(a little salt may be necessary)
fresh mint for garnish

Put all the mixed ingredients in a pan and simmer for 2 or 3 minutes. Serve cool, garnished with fresh mint, with warm, whole-wheat bread to mop up the sauce.

Escoffier's oyster mushrooms

This recipe is based on an old one which is reputed to have been devised by Escoffier. *Photograph opposite.*

12 oz/350 g oyster mushrooms
10 oz/275 g tomatoes, chopped
2 glasses white wine
2 shallots, finely chopped
1 clove garlic, finely chopped
2 tbsp oil
black pepper
1 cup parsley, chopped

Finely chop the shallots and garlic and soften in the oil. Clean and chop the mushrooms and cook on a high heat for 1 minute. Add the chopped tomato flesh and all the other ingredients. Cover and simmer gently for 30 minutes.

Stuffed mushrooms

8 large field mushrooms
8 tbsp breadcrumbs
1 oz/25 g margarine
1 egg yolk
4 tbsp *fromage blanc*
2 cloves garlic
4 oz/100 g diced smoked chicken (optional)
2 tbsp parsley, chopped
2 tbsp chives, chopped
pepper
SAUCE
½ pt/300 ml cheese sauce
1 oz/25 g breadcrumbs
Parmesan cheese

Page 107
Escoffier's oyster mushrooms

Wash the mushrooms, remove the stalks, and put in a shallow, ovenproof dish. Chop the stalks, crush the garlic, and mix with all the other ingredients. Fill the mushrooms caps with this mixture, coat with cheese sauce, sprinkle with more breadcrumbs and Parmesan, and bake in a medium oven for 15 minutes.

Pumpkin soup

I love the cheery sight of pumpkins on sale in the autumn, and I love to see parents making their children lanterns for Hallowe'en. I have grown them myself, and have happy memories of our lanterns on chilly Hallowe'en and Bonfire Night evenings. The flesh is always saved for a pie or soup, and this is one favourite recipe.

1 lb/450 g pumpkin
1 pt/600 ml chicken stock
1 tsp dill seed
a pinch of cinnamon
sugar to taste
pepper
fresh dill to garnish, if available
yoghurt
croûtons (see page 31)

Simmer all the ingredients together, except the dill herb and yoghurt, until the pumpkin is just cooked. Liquidize and serve with *croûtons*, yoghurt and the dill.

Artichoke vinaigrette

The globe artichoke is a handsome and very special vegetable, which we eat regularly throughout the year. It may be just an edible thistle but what a taste! Eating it is an occasion which can't be hurried. It has to be enjoyed leaf by leaf.

But we enjoy it most when it has grown in our own garden, because then it is smaller and tastier. It is also possible now to find small tender artichokes in the shops, which can be eaten whole.

Try to buy artichokes which are fresh, and which have not developed too much choke. Soak upside-down to remove insects, cut off the stalk, and boil for up to 30 minutes for a large vegetable.

4 large, globe artichokes
SAUCE
6 tbsp best olive oil
2 tbsp wine vinegar
marjoram, chopped
$\frac{1}{2}$ tsp French mustard
pepper

Combine the marjoram and mustard, and mix well. Cut off the stalks, pull off the outer leaves and trim the bases of the artichokes. Cut off the top of the leaves and cook in boiling, slightly salted water for about 20 minutes. The base should be slightly soft. Remove, refresh in cold water, drain and cool.

Serve each artichoke on a bed of varied salad leaves, with a small pot of the sauce. Put a sprig of fresh marjoram on the top of each artichoke.

Lemon artichoke creams

8 small, very young artichokes
1 pt/600 ml chicken stock
2 tbsp *fromage blanc*
juice of 1 lemon
black pepper to taste
lemon thyme (if available)

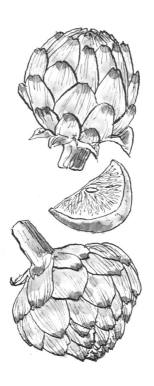

Cut off the top third of the artichokes. Take off the outer leaves until only light-green ones are left. Cover the artichokes with the stock, add pepper, and boil fast for about 10 minutes, when the stock should be well reduced. Put 2 artichokes into each of 4 small pots. Add the *fromage blanc*, lemon juice and a little chopped lemon thyme to the stock. Stir well, pour over the artichokes and serve garnished with sprigs of lemon thyme.

Goat's cheese and walnut salad

Use mixed salad leaves, including something bitter like chicory or dandelion. Also include oak leaf lettuce, to pick up the brown colour of the walnuts. Choose fresh walnuts if possible. *Photograph on page 123.*

2 oz/50 g walnuts, chopped
2 sharp eating apples (optional)
4 tbsp walnut oil
1 tbsp lemon juice
6 oz/175 g goat's cheese (you can use goat's cheese sold with walnuts incorporated in it)
black pepper

Scoop balls out of the apples, using a melon-baller. Arrange the salad leaves on 4 plates, scatter on apple balls and walnuts. Add the dressing of lemon juice and oil. Grill the goat's cheese, cut into 4 rounds, and when it is browned on top, lay on each plate of salad, and serve.

Stuffed tomatoes

4 beefsteak tomatoes
1 shallot
1 clove garlic
1 tbsp oil
½ tbsp tarragon
½ tbsp parsley
6 drops tabasco
3 tbsp pine kernels
4 tbsp cooked rice
pepper

Cut off the tops of the tomatoes and scoop out the pulp. Sieve and reserve. Soften the shallot and garlic in the oil and then mix in all the other ingredients, including the tomato pulp. Check the seasoning – you may want it spicier. Refill the tomatoes, bake in a medium oven for 30 minutes, and serve on a bed of salad leaves.

Basil and tomato sorbet

1 lb/450 g good tomatoes
a handful of basil leaves
a pinch of sugar
1 small clove garlic
2 egg-whites
pepper

Skin, seed and chop the tomatoes, purée and add pepper to taste. A pinch of sugar may be needed if they are not sweet enough. Add the puréed garlic and basil leaves to taste. Make the sorbet, adding the whisked egg-whites as described on page 61. Serve 1 sphere of sorbet, decorated with whole basil leaves, on a small white dish, as an appetizer before the main course.

Page 111
Basil and tomato sorbet

Stuffed aubergines

Aubergines are such a beautiful colour and shape that I am always reluctant to turn them into a purée, or use them as just one ingredient of a dish like mousaka. Their size is not important, but they must be eaten fresh. They are often tired in the shops, so check that they are firm.

Cooked the following way, they retain their shape, and can be served attractively on oval white dishes. This recipe makes the most of the aubergine's earthy taste and lovely texture.

2 large aubergines	**3 tbsp milk**
½ lb/225 g tomatoes	**1 tbsp marjoram, chopped**
1 clove garlic	**1 tbsp tomato purée**
6 anchovy fillets	**breadcrumbs**
a pinch of flour	**pepper**

Cut the aubergines in half lengthways, scoop out the flesh and cube it. Salt it, leave it to sweat, and then rinse away the salt an hour or so later. Heat the oil, and soften the vegetables well. Make a sauce from the crushed anchovy fillets, flour and milk, and add with the herbs and tomato purée to the vegetables. Cook until the mixture is no longer watery. Divide between the aubergine shells, season and scatter with the breadcrumbs. Bake in a medum oven for 30 minutes.

Vegetable terrine

In this recipe, broccoli can be used instead of spinach. Use just the stalks, saving the sprigs for a salad.

1 lb/450 g carrots
1 lb/450 g parsnips
1 lb/450 g spinach
pepper
2 tbsp lovage, chopped

Cook the vegetables separately for the normal length of time. Drain. Add pepper to taste to all of them, and add the lovage to the carrots. Purée all the vegetables and line a loaf-tin with foil. Spread a layer of each vegetable in turn. Cover and cook in a bain-marie in a low oven for 15 minutes. When it is set, serve in slices to show off the three different colours.

Duck liver salad

As chives and tomatoes are both used in this recipe, it is a perfect time to try the beautiful garnishing idea I saw in Orsi's restaurant in Lyons. Flowers are made from tomatoes, as explained on page 29, and the chives are used as stalks.

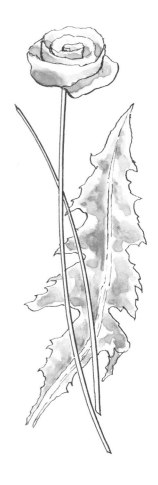

8 oz/225 g salad leaves, including a few dandelion, young spinach or curly endive to add a bitter taste
2 tomatoes, skinned and seeded
1 tbsp oil
6 oz/175 g duck livers
1 tbsp chives, chopped
pepper
DRESSING
1½ tbsp olive oil
½ tbsp white-wine vinegar
½ tsp French mustard
pepper

Arrange the washed salad leaves on 4 plates. Cut the tomatoes into strips and add to the salad along with the chives. Make a tomato and chive flower on each plate.

Season the livers and cook in the oil until browned on all sides, but pink in the middle. Arrange them on the salad and serve, with salad dressing handed separately.

Smoked salmon mousse

4 oz/100 g smoked salmon pieces
2 tbsp Quark
1 tbsp fennel, chopped
juice of 1 lemon or lime
pepper

This must be one of the easiest and quickest first courses to prepare, and I include it in my *Food of Love* because it is a tasty way of using up the pieces of smoked salmon after preparing recipes like the one on page 78. It really is a simple matter of blending these ingredients together in a food-processor, and arrange the mousse artistically on salad leaves, with fennel fronds and lemon or lime to garnish.

Quail and walnut salad

Quail are small and may make guests feel queasy. When I last bought quail at a London Sainsbury's, the girl on the check-out squealed: 'You don't eat those, do you?' A lot of people feel the same about pigeon. For me, the problem comes with anything smaller than quail. When I opened a tin of Chinese rice birds to discover they were less than one inch long, I felt horrified.

4 quail
4 tsp artichoke paste (optional)
4 nasturtium flowers
4 nasturtium leaves
1 head of oak leaf lettuce
4 walnut halves, chopped
2 tsp thyme, chopped
3 very small carrots, blanched
3 tbsp walnut oil
1 tbsp sherry vinegar
pepper

Rub the quail in a little oil, add the pepper and chopped thyme. Roast for 15 minutes in a hot oven. Serve whole on the following salad – or serve just the breasts.

Wash and dry the salad ingredients. Arrange a little oak leaf lettuce on each plate, plus 1 nasturtium leaf and flower. Cut the carrots into matchsticks and arrange attractively on each plate. Scatter the walnuts on the salad. Add 1 teaspoon of artichoke paste per plate. This can be bought in a jar, or made from puréed artichoke hearts. Make the dressing from the oil, thyme and vinegar. Pour over the salad. Add the hot quail and garnish with thyme.

Page 115
Quail and walnut salad

Pheasant pâté

This pâté can be made with any game. It is successful with pigeon, hare, rabbit and venison. With pheasant and pigeon, I often make it with the remaining flesh after using the breasts for a main course. Green peppercorns can be added to this recipe to make a pâté with real bite (half a teaspoon is about right). *Photograph on page 118.*

12 oz/350 g boned flesh from game
liver of the animal being used
6 oz/175 g lean bacon
1 egg
thyme
parsley
1 small onion, chopped
2 cloves garlic, crushed
1 tbsp oil
2 tbsp brandy
pepper
1 cup breadcrumbs

Soften the onion and garlic in the oil. Mince the game and bacon and then mix all the ingredients together. Pack into a 1½ pt/900 ml terrine. Bake in a medium oven, standing the terrine in water, for 1 to 1½ hours. It is best eaten 2 or 3 days later, when the full flavours have developed.

Scallops in a garden

This dish of raw, marinated scallops is excellent in the autumn when the freshest of home-grown vegetables are still available. All these vegetables should be cut into very fine julienne strips. Thinnings from the vegetable garden are excellent if you grow your own.

10 fresh scallops
handful of coriander leaves
1 inch/2.5 cm piece of fresh ginger root, peeled and cut into fine
    strips
3 oz/75 g each of mange-tout, courgettes, carrots, and any other
    baby vegetables available, like kohlrabi, and parsnips
4 oz/100 g natural yoghurt
juice of 1 lemon
pepper

Wash the scallops and slice them horizontally. Put them on a plate and marinate in the lemon juice, ginger, pepper and about half the coriander leaves, chopped. Leave for 4 hours or more. Cut the vegetables into strips. Mix each type with a little yoghurt and pepper. On each plate, put scallops in the centre, surrounded by piles of vegetables garnished with coriander.

Drunken scallops

Serve on salad leaves, like oak leaf lettuce, endive, lamb's tongue lettuce, radicchio, or nasturtium leaves. Scatter on sprouted seeds.

1 lb/450 g scallops
2 tbsp oil
2 cloves garlic, finely chopped
2 tsp tarragon vinegar
fresh tarragon and nasturtium flowers
1 glass dry vermouth
pepper

Wash the salad ingredients, dry, and arrange on an attractive serving dish. Wash the scallops and carefully scrape away the black line by the orange coral. Cook the garlic in the warm oil. Add the tarragon vinegar, chopped tarragon, vermouth and pepper. Add the scallops and cook in the liquid for 5 minutes, or until just cooked through. Remove and slice. Continue cooking the sauce until it is syrupy. Arrange the warm scallops on the salad and spoon over the sauce. Garnish with tarragon, and nasturtium flowers to pick up the orange colour of the coral.

Page 117
Pheasant pâté

MAIN COURSES

Skate in caper sauce

This curiously shaped fish, normally sold in pieces or 'wings', is in season from August to April. I am extremely fond of it, not just for its thick creamy flesh, but because it reminds me of a lovely fish-orientated holiday in Brittany. My eldest son, then four, loved skate *au beurre noir*. By the end of the holiday he had progressed to oysters, mussels, lobster and crab. This is my version of that Brittany skate, which started our family love affair for the fish.

4 pieces of skate
2 oz/50 g margarine
4 tbsp white-wine vinegar
1 tbsp capers
chopped chervil or parsley
pepper
1 onion

Simmer the skate for 20 minutes in water, flavoured with 1 glass of vinegar, the onion, mixed herbs and pepper. Remove, drain, and scrape away the skin from both sides. Serve with the sauce poured over it. This is prepared by warming the margarine with the wine vinegar and pepper. Add the capers and herbs at the last moment. Serve garnished with a sprig of fresh herb.

Skate with oranges and lemons

This is a more subtle sauce, served with the fish cooked as in the previous recipe. The sauce is made from the following ingredients.

2 shallots, chopped   **lemon thyme**
1 tbsp oil   **1 tsp white-wine vinegar**
1 orange   **pepper**
1 lemon

Page 119
Skate with orange and lemon

Soften the shallots in the oil. Peel the fruit. Cut half of the orange and half of the lemon into slices, and use the other halves to make juice. Add the juice, vinegar, 1 teaspoon of chopped thyme, pepper and a little finely grated and blanched fruit peel to the pan. Boil up. Heat through the orange and lemon slices and arrange on the fish artistically. Pour over the sauce and garnish with lemon thyme.

Trout with banana and ginger stuffing

4 trout
1 small onion, finely chopped
1 clove garlic, finely chopped
1 tbsp oil
1 tbsp coriander, chopped
2 tbsp walnuts, chopped
1 inch/2.5 cm piece of root ginger, grated
2 tbsp celery, chopped
1 chopped spring onion and 4 for garnish
1 banana, chopped
pepper
coriander to garnish

Soften the onion, then the garlic and celery in the oil. Then add the ginger and spring onion and cook for 2 or 3 minutes. Mix with the pepper, banana and nuts. Stuff the prepared trout, and bake in a hot oven for 15 minutes. Serve with new potatoes and salad, garnished with lemon, spring onion tassels (See page 28) and coriander.

Monkfish marinade

2 lb/900 g monkfish, cubed
2 sweet peppers, 1 green, 1 red or yellow
2 oz/50 g button mushrooms
1 small onion, cut into chunks
MARINADE
1 inch/2.5 cm piece of root ginger, grated
1 fresh chilli, chopped
2 cloves garlic, chopped
2 tsp coriander
3 tbsp lemon juice
8 oz/225 g natural yoghurt
1 tsp ground cumin
coriander and lemon for garnish

Mix the marinade ingredients together. Add the fish and leave for at least 1 hour. Put on skewers, alternating with pieces of onion, button mushrooms and at least 2 colous of sweet peppers. Grill each side for about 10 minutes. Garnish with coriander and lemon, and serve with brown rice, and the marinade heated through as a sauce.

Kidneys with lemon garlic

This dish is quick and easy to make, but it is unusually refreshing. Serve on a bed of fresh spinach or, if preferred, with brown rice and salad.

8 lambs' kidneys
1 tbsp oil
6 large cloves garlic
juice of 1 lemon
black pepper
lemon thyme
1 lemon for garnish

Skin and core the kidneys before cutting into $\frac{1}{2}$-inch/1-cm pieces. Chop the garlic and herbs, and fry with the kidneys and pepper in hot oil for about 5 minutes. Add the lemon juice and serve as the juices run out of the kidneys. Garnish with lemon and sprigs of lemon thyme.

Sweetbreads with herbs

1 lb/450 g sweetbreads, calves' or lambs'
1 glass white wine
2 shallots, chopped
1 clove garlic
4 oz/100 g button mushrooms, sliced
2 tbsp *fromage blanc*
1 tbsp oil
light stock
bunch fresh herbs, chopped
pepper

*Page 123
Sweetbreads with herbs.
Goat's cheese with walnut
salad*

Cover sweetbreads with water for 1 hour. Then cook briefly in the light stock and leave to cool. Slice, ready to use. Soften the shallots and garlic in oil, add the mushrooms for 1 minute, then the wine, the fresh herbs (marjoram is good with sweetbreads), the sweetbreads and enough stock to cover, and simmer until tender. Sweetbreads need very little cooking. Season. Assemble the sliced sweetbreads on a plate, thicken the sauce with *fromage blanc*, check seasoning, pour over the sweetbreads and garnish with fresh herbs. Serve with a green vegetable and new potatoes.

Sweetbreads with walnut sauce

I also make a similar dish, using ceps instead of walnuts. The strong flavour of these most special fungi is excellent with sweetbreads.

1 lb/450 g calves' sweetbreads
lemon juice
1 onion, finely chopped
1 clove garlic, finely chopped
1 tbsp oil
1 tbsp parsley

1 glass white wine
2 tbsp chicken stock
4 oz/100 g walnuts, pounded
2 tbsp *fromage blanc*
pepper
parsley to garnish

Soak the sweetbreads in water for 1 hour. Rinse and then simmer in water with lemon juice for several minutes. Then put in cold water, remove the fat and leave to cool between plates with a heavy weight on top. Soften the onion and garlic in the oil, add the wine, parsley and stock, and then the sweetbreads and cook gently for about 15 minutes. Then put in 3 oz/75 g of the pounded walnuts, and simmer for about 5 minutes to let the flavour of the walnuts develop. Thicken with *fromage blanc*, and serve garnished with walnuts and parsley.

Sour quince chicken

It is traditional in many countries to cook chicken in vinegar to produce an unusual but very special sour taste. I have made the Persian version myself with wine vinegar, but prefer this sour chicken, using lots of garlic, quince, and dry wine, to achieve a similar result.

1 large fresh chicken
4 cloves garlic
$\frac{1}{2}$ lemon
black pepper
paprika

1 bay-leaf
$\frac{1}{2}$ pt/150 ml dry white wine
2 quince, sliced
1 tbsp oil

Put slivers of garlic under the chicken's skin. Rub the lemon juice all over the bird, and then put the shell and bay-leaf in the chicken's cavity. Sprinkle with the paprika and black pepper. Heat the oil in a casserole and brown the chicken in it. Add the quince and the wine, put on the lid, and cook in a medium oven for 1 to $1\frac{1}{2}$ hours. Remove the chicken, keep warm, and reduce the juices to the ideal consistency. Serve with brown rice and a crisp green salad.

Guinea-fowl with lovage and lime

This dish has a memorable flavour, which only lovage can provide. It can be made at any time of the year, even using dried lovage in winter. But it is best to make it in the autumn, when the lovage leaves have not died back, but are not fresh enough to chop up in salads.

1 hen guinea-fowl	2 tbsp dry Martini
1 oz/25 g margarine	4 tbsp *fromage frais*
1 onion, chopped	juice of $\frac{1}{2}$ lime
1 clove garlic, chopped	$\frac{1}{4}$ pt/150 ml chicken stock
5 sprigs lovage	pepper

Melt the margarine in a large casserole and brown the bird. Take it out and soften the onion and garlic in the casserole. Put the sprigs of lovage on top of the onion, replace the guinea-fowl, pour over the stock and Martini, season and cook gently for about an hour. When the bird is tender, put it on a serving dish, remove the fat from the juices in the casserole and take out the lovage. Add the *fromage frais* and lime juice. Simmer until a good consistency and check the sauce to see if it needs more pepper or lime juice. Serve with the sauce, potatoes in their skins and a subtle green vegetable, like broccoli.

Garnish the guinea-fowl with lime butterflies or cones (see page 30) and fresh lovage. *Photograph on page 126.*

Calf's liver with orange

8 small slices liver	cayenne
1 onion, chopped	2 tbsp oil
2 cloves garlic, crushed	cup of stock
2 tbsp flour	a little red wine
black pepper	parsley
dry mustard	
thyme (lemon thyme preferably)	
2 oranges, 1 sliced for garnish and 1 for juice and peel	

Page 126
Guinea fowl with lovage and lime

Add some grated and blanched orange peel, a pinch of mustard, cayenne and black pepper to the flour. Roll the liver in it. Fry it in the oil. Take out and keep warm. Now add the onion and garlic to the juices and oil. Cook slowly until golden. Add the stock, orange juice, wine and herbs. Cook till a good consistency, and then spoon over the liver. Serve with brown rice, and garnish with orange and fresh herbs.

Pigeons with apricot sauce

Although I have several ways of cooking whole pigeons, I do prefer to use just the breasts in main courses. Then I put the carcass in water to produce game stock. The flesh can also be used for game pâté (see page 116) or soup. The following recipe uses lightly cooked pigeon breasts with a rich and interesting sauce. *Photograph on page 127.*

4 pigeon
5 oz/150 g dried apricots
3 oz/75 g margarine
2 shallots, chopped
½ pt/150 ml good stock
1 glass brandy
pepper
pinch lemon thyme

Heat the oven. Melt 1 oz/25 g margarine in a pan, brown the peppered pigeons and cook in a hot oven for 10 minutes. Remove the breasts and keep the rest of the birds for making pâté. Soften the shallots in the rest of the margarine, add the soaked and softened apricots, stock, and pepper, with a pinch of fresh lemon thyme. Simmer the sauce, while warming the breasts through in a pan with the juices from the oven cooking. Deglaze the pan with brandy, add a little stock and simmer. Purée the apricot sauce, place the pigeon breasts 2 to a plate, add the brandy juices to the apricot sauce and pour a little over the pigeon breasts. Serve the pigeon on individual plates with new potatoes, French beans and carrot and lovage purée (see page 132).

Page 127
Pigeons with apricot sauce

Pigeons with grapes

Doves were sacred to Aphrodite, and far too special to eat. I think most of us would agree today, although we are far less fussy about the related wood pigeon. Some people stil feel strange eating such a small, common bird. But do not be scrupulous, because they are pests and farmers have to reduce their numbers. They are extremely tasty too. Although they are in season throughout the year, they are at their best from August to October. I cook them in many ways: casseroled with green olives and red wine; with 20 cloves of garlic; or, in the summer, cold in aspic with cherries. This recipe is a favourite.

4 young pigeons
thyme
1 bay-leaf
1 small onion, chopped
1 clove garlic, chopped
1 lb/450 g firm, seedless grapes, halved
1 tbsp brandy
1 tbsp oil
1 cup of game or beef stock
pepper

Cut the pigeons in half lengthways, and brown in hot oil with the onion. Flame with brandy, add the herbs, seasoning, stock and grapes. Cover with foil and a tight lid and cook in a medium oven until the birds are tender, probably at least an hour. Serve with grape sauce, which should be checked for seasoning and reduced, if necessary, before serving.

Duck with elderberry sauce

Wild duck is less fatty than farmed duck, so as it is only possible to buy whole birds, you can remove the breasts and then use the rest of the bird for making pâté or soup. But lean, farmed duck breasts are now readily available, which can be grilled under a high heat to reduce the fat content. These are ideal for this particular recipe if wild duck is not available. Also, take care with wild birds because they can be tough and may need longer and more gentle cooking.

4 duck breasts
3 tbsp *Crème de Cassis*
10 oz/275 g elderberries
3 oz/75 g or more sugar, depending on the sweetness
    of the elderberries
$\frac{1}{4}$ pt/150 ml chicken stock, or duck stock if available

Start by seasoning the breasts well with pepper. Once the sauce has been prepared, grill for just a few minutes on each side, so they are well-done on the outside but still pink in the middle.

Make the sauce by washing and removing the elderberries from their stalks and simmering in the stock for about 20 minutes. Taste to see if the sauce needs a little sugar, reduce to a good consistency, add the *Cassis*, and pour over the duck breasts. Garnish with a few fresh berries.

129

Venison with herbs

Venison is very special. It is in season from June to January. This recipe uses 1 large leg of venison, marinaded for 2 days in the following mixture: yoghurt snow flavoured with kirsch (see page 65).

MARINADE

½ pt/300 ml red wine

handful of mixed, chopped parsley, marjoram, thyme, rosemary and sage

1 onion, 1 stick of celery, 1 carrot, 1 clove garlic, all softened in 1 oz/25 g margarine

2 tbsp oil

1 onion, chopped

2 carrots, chopped

1 leek, chopped

1 parnsip, chopped

4 sage leaves

8 juniper berries

black pepper

1 tbsp thyme

1 tbsp parsley

1 tbsp marjoram

1 tbsp rosemary

½ pt/300 ml good stock

2 tbsp red currant jelly

After 2 days, remove the venison from the marinade, dry and brown in the oil. Put it on a bed of the vegetables and herbs. Add the stock. Strain the marinade and add to the stock and slowly roast, for about 3 hours, in a medium oven. Turn and baste frequently. Remove the meat and carve it thickly. Discard the herbs from the base, then purée the vegetables and add the red currant jelly to produce a thick sauce. Serve with baked potatoes and crisp vegetables. *Photograph opposite.*

Page 131
Venison with herbs

VEGETABLES

Juniper potatoes

2 lb/900 g potatoes
3 tbsp oil
20 juniper berries, crushed
3 tbsp parsley, chopped
pepper

Peel and grate the potatoes, rinse and drain. Heat them in the hot oil with the pepper and juniper berries. When cooked, add the parsley and mix in with the potatoes. Good with pheasant and venison.

Carrots with lovage

1 lb/450 g carrots
2 tbsp margarine
2 tbsp chicken stock
1 clove garlic, finely chopped
1 onion, chopped
1 tbsp lovage, chopped
seasoning

Cut the washed carrots into thin slices. Melt the margarine and add the carrots, onion, garlic and lovage. Season with pepper, add the stock, cover and cook for 6 minutes or until the carrots are tender. Check the seasoning just before serving. This is also excellent as a purée.

PUDDINGS

WALNUTS

We are lucky enough to have a huge walnut tree in our tiny back garden in London. And we have always made full use of it. In the summer, when the fruits are still fleshy, before the nuts form, we pick them for pickling, using a recipe from Mrs Beaton's old book. The green fruits have to be pricked all over, put in brine solution, which has to be changed regularly, and then left to blacken in the sun before being pickled. We really enjoy coping with our walnut harvest, and our friends enjoy receiving jars of these very special pickles. I have never been able to find many recipes which use pickled walnuts, although of course they are marvellous eaten simply with bread and cheese. But I have made a Victorian recipe of beef with pickled walnuts, and at Christmas I use them to stuff goose, as I explain on page 172.

Some of the fruits must be left on the tree to develop into nuts, because fresh walnuts taste so much better then the normal, dried nuts which sell so well at Christmas-time. I was not aware of the great difference until a new window-cleaner arrived and asked if he could use his ladder to pick some of our walnuts. He appreciated the fresh taste of walnuts taken from the tree, and from then on I did too. The French have always been interested in fresh nuts, like walnuts, in the autumn. On a recent trip to Lyons in October, I found the markets and restaurants full of fresh walnuts, and a few good greengrocers stock them in Britain too. So if you find walnuts selling in October, check that they are fresh, and try them. They are beautiful, eaten on their own after a meal, or perhaps cooked with chicken (page 85) with Jerusalem artichokes (page 150), in walnut soup, as a stuffing for prunes, or with apricots as in the following recipe.

Apricot and walnut crumble

6 oz/175 g dried apricots, soaked overnight
10 oz/275 g sharp eating apples, peeled and sliced
2 oz/50 g sugar   4 oz/100 g fresh walnuts, shelled and chopped

Arrange in a pie dish, and top with the following crumble mixture:

4 oz/100 g margarine   2 oz/50 g more chopped walnuts
8 oz/225 g flour   2 tbsp sugar

Make a crumble with the margarine and flour. Cover the fruit with it and put sugar and walnuts on top. Bake in a medium oven for 30 to 45 minutes.

PEARS

Pears are another pleasure of autumn, which I enjoy in savoury and sweet dishes. Try sliced pears with a blue cheese or watercress sauce as a starter. And raw pears are excellent with the last raspberries of the season, or cooked with lots of spices and wine. But perfect pears are difficult to find in the shops. So often they are too hard, or bruised. The only really sure way of checking their condition is to eat one before buying, although you do need to have an understanding greengrocer before you try this. Perfect pears can be peeled, leaving the stalk, and then cored. The hollow centre should be filled with a mixture of walnuts (chopped finely), honey, and *fromage blanc*. Then the pears should be served on a pool of raspberry sauce, garnished with whole raspberries and a few chopped walnuts. Use fresh walnuts for this recipe if you can find them. Perfect pears and perfect walnuts are both sold in the autumn months.

If your pears are far-from perfect, then cook them instead. I have one pear tree which produces a lot of hard and small pears. So I use them in various recipes which poach fruit.

Pears in red wine

2 lb/900 g small pears
juice of 1 lemon
6 oz/175 g sugar
$\frac{3}{4}$ pt/450 ml water
pinch powdered cinnamon
orange and lemon peel
$\frac{1}{2}$ pt/300 ml red wine

Peel the pears, but do not core them. Boil the spices, sugar and peel in the water. Add the pears and simmer for 15 minutes. Pour in red wine and simmer for another 10 minutes or more, until the pears are really tender. Arrange the pears in a serving dish, and then reduce the syrup until it is a good consistency. Pour over the pears, chill, and serve with yoghurt snow flavoured with Kirsch (see page 65).

Apple turnover

8 oz/225 g wholemeal puff pastry (this can
   be bought frozen)
6 medium dessert apples, preferably sharp tasting
3 small quince (optional)
juice of half a lemon
4 oz/100 g margarine
5 oz/150 g sugar

Heat the oven. While it is getting hot, peel, core and halve the apples.
Pour over the lemon juice to prevent them discolouring. Grease the
base of a round, heatproof dish with margarine. Cover the bottom with
sugar and arrange the apple halves, rounded side down. In the hollows
left by the removal of the cores, put a slice of quince.

Roll out the puff pastry into a circle, lay it on top of the apples,
allowing an overlap all round the dish. Trim off the excess. Put the pan
on a hot ring for 10 minutes to darken the sugar, and then cook in a
medium oven for about 20 minutes, or until the golden pastry rises.

Serve it, by turning it over so the pastry is as the bottom of the dish,
the apples on top. Serve very hot with thick plain yoghurt.

Apple snow

A more ambitious and unusual pudding can be tried in the autumn by
adding 6 oz/175 g of home-made rose-hip syrup to the apple mixture.
This can be made by crushing 1 lb/450 g of bright-orange hips and
boiling them for 15 minutes in $1\frac{1}{2}$ pt/900 ml of water. Strain, boil again
and strain. Reduce the final liquid until it is syrupy.

10 crisp eating apples   3 egg-whites
1 tsp cinnamon   6 oz/175 g castor sugar
1 oz/25 g muscovado sugar   grated rind of 1 lemon
juice of 1 lemon   2 oz/50 g flaked almonds
a little water

Cook the prepared apple pieces until soft in a mixture of the water,
cinnamon, muscovado sugar and lemon juice. Then make the snow.
Whisk the egg-whites until stiff, add most of the castor sugar, the lemon
rind and the nuts. Put on top of the stewed, cool, apples, sprinkle with a
little of the remaining sugar and bake for about 15 minutes, when the
meringue should be brown. Serve with yoghurt snow (see page 65).

Apple streusal

Although I normally make apple streusal with filo pastry, this flan is useful for a more substantial pudding. It is extremely tasty, served with plain, thick yoghurt.

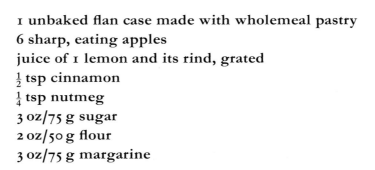

1 unbaked flan case made with wholemeal pastry
6 sharp, eating apples
juice of 1 lemon and its rind, grated
$\frac{1}{2}$ tsp cinnamon
$\frac{1}{4}$ tsp nutmeg
3 oz/75 g sugar
2 oz/50 g flour
3 oz/75 g margarine

Peel the apples, cut into pieces, cover in lemon juice and arrange on the flan case. Sprinkle over the spices. Combine the sugar, lemon rind, flour and margarine until crumbly. Put on top of the apple flan and bake in a hot oven for 30 minutes. Garnish with apple slices in the centre, and lemon butterflies (see page 30).

A passionate purée of autumn fruits

6 oz/175 g blackberries, cooked and cooled
8 oz/225 g apples, peeled, cored and cooked
1 mango
4 kiwi fruits
6 oz/175 g late strawberries
lemon juice
mint to garnish
sugar (optional)

Purée and sieve all the fruits separately. Thin with water if necessary, and add a little sugar or lemon juice if needed. Chill. Serve in individual bowls by putting a scoop of blackberry purée in the centre, surrounded by 1 scoop of each of the other 4 fruit purées. Shake the bowl slightly, so the purées mix a little at their meeting points. Garnish with whole strawberries and mint.

Green grape jelly

I have a five-year-old vine in the conservatory which now produces plenty of grapes, as well as useful shade. I use the leaves to stuff, in Greek-style, but the grapes are too small and full of pips to eat raw. So these are transformed in the early autumn into a beautiful grape jelly.

2 lb/900 g green grapes
1 pt/600 ml water
a handful of sweet cicely leaves
2 small packets of gelatine

Soften the grapes by simmering in the water with the sweet cicely leaves, which add a naturally sweet flavour. Leave to cool, then liquidize and sieve. Add the gelatine in the normal way, and leave the jelly to set in an attractive mould. I have several ornate Victorian moulds which are perfect for special jellies. Fresh fruit, like kiwi, or peeled, halved green grapes, can be added to the jelly to make it even more special. Serve with attractive fresh fruits, garnished with sweet cicely.

Elderberry sorbet

For every $\frac{1}{2}$ pt/300 ml of fruit juice:
4 oz/100 g sugar
4 cloves
1 tbsp *Crème de Cassis*
2 egg-whites

First make an elderberry syrup by picking the fruit, washing it well, and snipping off the berries from the stems. Put it in a pan with just enough water to cover, and simmer for 30 minutes. Sieve. Add the sugar and the cloves. Heat until the sugar is dissolved. Boil for 10 minutes and cool. Add the *Crème de Cassis*. Make into a sorbet in the normal way, using the whipped egg-whites. This sorbet has an interesting taste, and looks particularly beautiful served with an ice-cream and fresh fruits, garnished with elderberries. One successful autumn combination is to serve this sorbet with quince ice-cream (see below) and blackberries lightly cooked in a *Cassis* sauce. Use the elderberry syrup with the following sorbet, which can also be made in the autumn, as these imported fruits are available.

137

Passion-fruit sorbet

6 passion-fruit
2 egg whites

Cut the fruit in half and remove the flesh with a teaspoon. Purée the flesh, taste it to see if it needs any sugar, and then make a sorbet in the normal way, using stiffly whisked egg-whites. Serve with the elderberry sauce heated with at least 1 tablespoon of *Cassis*.

Quince ice-cream

8 quince, peeled and sliced
4 bananas
1 glass white wine
$\frac{1}{2}$ pt/300 ml yoghurt
1 cup milk
3 tbsp honey

Soften the quince in the simmering milk. Cool the fruit and purée the mixture of ingredients before making this ice-cream in the normal way, as described on page 64.

The grand finale of taste

This is a very special way of serving a little of the raspberry ice-cream, mango ice-cream and lemon, elderberry or pineapple sorbets of the previous recipes.

Put a little of each on 4 plates, pour a little mango sauce between them and garnish with fresh raspberries or late strawberries and mint leaves. The mango sauce is made by puréeing 1 ripe mango with the juice of 1 lemon.

Page 139
Sorbets and ice-creams

PRESERVES

To have a cupboard full of exotic preserves makes it easier to turn out exotic meals quickly. Pork fillet with my spiced quince as garnish, and roast pheasant with the following whole spiced crab-apples, are just two examples. As I have a crab-apple tree in the garden, which produces lovely, tiny yellow and red fruits, I increase the quantities in the recipe substantially. But many people may prefer to make a small sample to start with. Crab-apples are sold by some shops, but they are also seen growing wild by the roadside. Bottles of preserves make perfect presents for birthdays and Christmas.

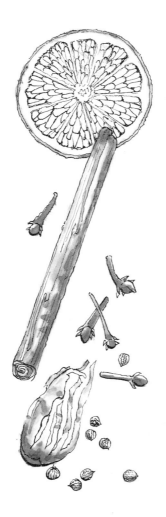

Spiced quince or oranges

This basic recipe for cooking fruit as a preserve in a vinegar brew is successful with oranges or quince, if you can get your hands on enough of them. I have both the quince shrub, which produces fruit the size of walnuts, and the more unusual tree, which grows pear-like quince. So I not only use this lovely fruit in many recipes, I have enough to give away to friends.

12 oranges or 12 large quince (30 small ones would be needed)
2 lb/900 g sugar
1 pt/600 ml red-wine vinegar
1 tsp mace
2 tsp coriander seeds
1 cinnamon stick
1 tsp cloves

Slice the fruit, having peeled and cored the quince. The oranges are sliced whole, and only the seeds removed. Simmer the oranges for 30 minutes in water to remove some of the bitterness. Do *not* do this with quince. Mix all the other ingredients together and bring to the boil. Simmer the quince or orange slices covered, until they are soft, but still intact. Leave in the juices for a day. Then bring to the boil again, and bottle in the normal way. The preserved fruit will be at its best after 2 months. If you are giving bottles as presents, checked-gingham is pretty to cover the lids. Use red and white at Christmas, and tie with a red ribbon trimmed with holly. The green and yellow ginghams are good at other times, with matching ribbons. Try yellow with lemon curd, and green with herb jellies.

Spiced crab-apples

1 lb/450 g small crab-apples
8 oz/225 g sugar
3 tbsp white-wine vinegar
several cloves
1 cinnamon stick
several black peppercorns
several coriander seeds
$\frac{1}{2}$ pt/300 ml cold water

Wash the apples and remove the stalks. Put the fruit in a pan. Make a syrup with the sugar, water, vinegar and spices. Bring to the boil until the sugar has dissolved and the syrup thickened: 45 minutes is usually right. Add to the apples in their pan, and simmer until soft. If they are small, this will only take a few minutes. Take care not to soften them too much. They can suddenly lose their shape. Skim the surface and put into clean, dry jars. Seal.

WINTER

Winter is my least favourite season, so good food is needed to cheer it up. A perfect winter weekend day is to go to a 'real' pub in the Cotswolds with my family and dogs. A drink and a snack in front of the log fire are followed by a five- or six-mile walk. On the way home, we call at the game shop and buy pheasant, venison, pigeon or whatever else is available, not only for that evening, but for the rest of the week too.

This is the time to dig up our never-ending supply of Jerusalem artichokes, which have been given away in previous years to spread in several gardens belonging to friends. Finding new ways of cooking them is one of the challenges of winter. My three favourite ideas are to make soup, finished off with scallops; to cook them in walnut oil with shallots and nuts; or to serve them cold in a dressing with prawns.

Leeks are also grown for winter, and as my recipes prove, these are one of my very favourite vegetables. Seville oranges make their brief appearance, and I snap them up, not only for marmalade, but to make the special sour sauce to eat with roast duck. All the citrus fruits are excellent at this time of the year, through to the spring. It is good to end a heavy meal with sorbets made from grapefruit, lemon and orange. I also love these sorbets between savoury courses, during a long and special meal, like the gourmet dinner we enjoyed on my fortieth birthday in Monte Carlo. Splendid course followed splendid course, and we only coped with all this excess because our palates were revived with a subtle grapefruit sorbet. Sorbets look their best served in the hollowed-out shells of the fruit.

Winter is the time to cheer people up by inviting them around for long and lovely meals. It is good occasionally to serve a feast from other countries, like Greece. I would also love one day to recreate one of those seasonal meals of Mrs Beaton's, with perhaps a dozen courses. We have decided that when we do this we will make the meal last the whole weekend, and we will invite friends to eat different parts of the meal at different times. Can you imagine the invitation? 'Can you come round for pudding at noon, Sunday, please?'

STARTERS

MUSSELS

Mussels provide us with the cheapest opportunity to enjoy the sweet succulence and fresh taste of the sea that shellfish bring. They are such a bargain, compared to other seafoods, that it seems such a pity that many people only taste them in vinegar. I have collected them myself off the rocks around our coast, and find that the small ones taste so much better than the large mussels sold in shops. But you do have to be careful that they are not collected from polluted areas. And remember that there are far too many sewage outlets around the British coast than there should be.

We had a bit of a laugh collecting mussels one year when there had been a pollution scare on the North-East coast, called the Red Tide. People who had eaten seafood in the polluted area had suffered temporary paralysis. So when we were on holiday soon after on the South Coast at Broadstairs, we decided to check with the Local Health Authority about any pollution problems in the area. We had found masses of mussels on the Broadstairs beach and rang up the Health Inspector to see if they were safe. 'You want to eat local mussels?' he said in amusement. 'Nobody does that around Broadstairs. You'd better ring up Ramsgate, it's the sort of thing they do there.' Despite his snobbery, we decided to chance it, and the mussels were delicious.

Although I love eating mussels, I loathe cleaning them. I find the best way is to scrub them under a running cold tap, scraping off the beard and bits sticking to the shells. Open and broken ones are thrown away, and I then cook them over heat, usually in wine, for 5 minutes. I like them in soups, baked with a herb butter, hot on a salad base, in paella, and with pasta. Perhaps they are at their most glamorous served with home-made black pasta, a recipe inspired by my friend Antonio Carluccio.

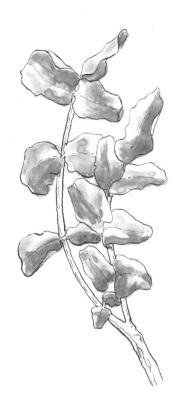

Page 143
Mussel soup

Watercress soup with mussels

1 lb/450 g mussels
1 small onion, peeled and chopped
1 clove garlic, peeled and chopped
1 large leek, cleaned and chopped
3 large potatoes, chopped
1 bunch watercress
1 tbsp oil

1½ pt/900 ml chicken stock
1 glass dry white wine
1 tbsp chopped thyme
pepper

Soften all vegetables in the oil, putting a few watercress leaves aside for garnish. Add the stock and simmer for about 10 minutes, until the potatoes are soft. Purée and season. Wash and prepare the mussels, add to the pan with the wine and thyme. Cook until the mussels open; throw away those that don't open in cooking. Remove the shells, and add the mussels, plus the herbs and wine, to the soup. Serve warm with watercress leaves as a garnish. *Photograph on page 143.*

Moules marinière

For a change, try thickening the sauce with 2 tablespoons of *fromage blanc*. Fennel can also be used instead of the mixed herbs, to add an aniseed taste.

About 40 mussels, washed and scraped
1 large onion, chopped
2 tbsp parsley, chopped
sprig of thyme
1 bay-leaf
2 glasses white wine
a little oil
pepper

Cook the onion in hot oil until transparent. Add the wine and herbs and simmer for 10 minutes. Add the mussels to the wine in the saucepan, cover with the lid and steam until all the shells open. Put the mussels in a large bowl, while you reduce the liquid to half, then pour over them. Garnish with fresh parsley and serve with wholemeal bread.

Fish and fennel soup

1 lb/450 g fish trimmings
1 onion, sliced
1 fennel bulb
bouquet garni
juice of 2 lemons

12 fennel seeds
12 peppercorns
8 coriander seeds
1 egg yolk

Put everything, but the egg and lemon, into a pan. Cover with water and simmer for 40 minutes. Strain. Adjust seasoning, add the lemon juice and whisk in the egg yolk carefully, making sure it does not curdle.

Leek salad with prawns and quail's eggs

Leeks are one of the oldest of all vegetables, and they are one of my favourites. In the North-East of England, where my family comes from, the leek is king, the star of the vegetable shows which have prizes like suites of furniture for the best on offer. The secret formulae make them grow to enormous dimensions – but they tend to have very little taste. So now that I grow my own leeks, I pull them up fairly small. They taste so exquisite that we eat them raw. I serve them cooked, cooled and covered in French dressing. I use them in pasta sauces, as a filling for flans and in many soups, including the famous Vichyssoise. Leeks are also excellent in salads, as I hope this recipe proves.

8 quail's eggs
12 thin leeks
24 prawns
French dressing (see page 73)
1 lemon
12 tiny tomatoes, halved
tarragon

*Page 147
Leek salad with prawns and
quail's eggs*

Cook the leeks until tender, drain and leave to cool in the French dressing overnight. Slice the leeks and divide between 4 individual plates, arranging the vegetable in a star shape. Put 1 lightly cooked egg in its shell in the centre of the star, with another egg, shelled and cut into 4, arranged around it. Arrange the prawns and tomatoes in a circle between the leeks, sprinkle over the lemon juice and chopped tarragon, and garnish with tarragon and lemon twists. *Photograph opposite.*

French onion soup

This is a popular winter soup in our family, reminding us of happy holidays spent in France, near Lake Geneva, where a favourite restaurant serves a particularly good version of this traditional soup.

1 lb/450 g onions, chopped   2 tbsp grated Parmesan
1 tbsp oil   2 tbsp grated Gruyère cheese
1½ pt/900 ml good chicken stock   pepper
½ wholemeal French loaf   a little chopped thyme

Cook the onions until brown in the oil. Then add the stock and thyme, and simmer for 20 minutes or so. Adjust the seasoning, add slices of bread to the casserole with the soup, sprinkle cheese on top, and put in the oven until well browned.

Game soup

I use game, like partridge, pheasant, pigeon or grouse, left after the breasts have been removed, to cook for a main course.

1 game bird
1 tbsp oil
2 onions
2 flat mushrooms
2 carrots
2 celery sticks
1 bay-leaf
thyme
2 pt/1 l chicken or game stock
1 glass wine
1 tbsp red currant jelly
juice of ½ lemon
parsley, chopped

Brown the bird in the oil. Remove, then brown the vegetables. Replace the bird and all the other ingredients and simmer for at least an hour. Take the meat off the bird and put aside. Liquidize the soup, add the red currant jelly and lemon juice, and adjust the seasoning. Put in the sliced meat, heat through and serve garnishedwith chopped parsley.

Celeriac and carrot soup

1 large celeriac, weighing about 1 lb/450 g
½ lb/225 g carrots
1½ pt/900 ml chicken stock
1 tbsp oil
seasoning
chopped lovage, or parsley if not available
a little yoghurt

Cook the chopped celeriac and carrots in oil till soft, then simmer in the stock until tender. Purée the result, add the other ingredients and serve.

Jerusalem artichoke soup

2 lb/900 g artichokes, peeled and sliced
2 onions, chopped
1 clove garlic
2 tbsp oil
1½ pt/900 ml chicken stock
½ pt/300 ml skimmed milk
pepper
some salt or salt substitute will be needed
***fromage blanc* and *croûtons* for garnish**

Soften the onions and garlic in the oil, add the artichokes and simmer in the milk for 10 minutes. Then add the stock and seasoning, and simmer for 15 minutes. Liquidize, adjust the seasoning and serve with a swirl of *fromage blanc* and toasted, wholemeal *croûtons*. This is one vegetable that always needs some salt or substitute to bring out its wonderful flavour.

Scallop and artichoke soup

For a more special soup, add 8 sliced scallops, which have been poached in dry white wine, to the soup just before serving. Garnish with tarragon. *Photograph on page 151.*

Artichoke and walnut timbales

1½ lb/700 g Jerusalem artichokes
4 oz/100 g walnuts
½ lb/225 g spinach
4 fl oz/100 ml milk
4 eggs, beaten

1 oz/25 g margarine
1 pt/600 ml chicken stock
pepper
basil or parsley for garnish

SAUCE
½ lb/225 g tomatoes, chopped
1 orange
1 tbsp red-wine vinegar

basil to taste
pepper

The *timbales* are cooked in individual ramekins which should be greased with the margarine. Peel the artichokes and cook them in the chicken stock for about 10 minutes. Drain and keep the liquid. Cook the spinach for 10 minutes and drain. Purée the vegetables together and add most of the walnuts, pounded. When cool, mix with the milk, pepper, ⅓ pint/200 ml of the artichoke liquid, and the eggs. Mix well, pour into the ramekins, put foil over the surfaces and cook in a bain-marie in a medium oven for about 45 minutes. Turn out, garnish with chopped nuts and basil or parsley, and surround with the hot tomato and orange sauce. This is made by simmering the tomatoes in a little oil, sieving them and heating them through with the orange juice, wine vinegar, pepper and basil. *Photograph opposite.*

Artichoke and seafood salad

1 lb/450 g Jerusalem artichokes
6 tbsp olive oil
2 tbsp lemon juice
4 oz/100 g shelled prawns
12 cooked mussels
1 cup chives, chopped
½ inch/1 cm piece of root ginger, grated
pepper

Page 151
Scallops and artichoke soup.
Artichoke and walnut
timbales

Boil and slice the artichokes. Leave to cool in a dressing made from the oil, lemon juice and pepper. Arrange on an oval, white dish with the prawns, mussels, grated ginger and chives. If chive flowers are still growing in the herb garden, they pick up the pink of the prawns beautifully.

Haddock mousse

Winter is the best time of the year for young haddock, and smoked haddock is particularly succulent. It can be used to make many interesting fish courses. Pretty individual moulds can be used to make this cheery, fish mousse. If the moulds have a relief design, this can first be filled with chopped parsley.

8 oz/225 g smoked haddock, flaked
2 shallots, chopped
2 oz/50 g margarine
2 eggs
parsley, chopped
1 oz/25 g Parmesan cheese
3 fl oz/75 ml milk
pepper

Soften the shallots in the margarine, and then mix in the fish, pepper and milk. Blend. Chill for an hour. Grease the moulds, sprinkle the parsley into the relief shapes at the bottom. Add the beaten egg yolks and cheese into the fish mixture, then add the stiffly beaten egg-whites. Pour into the moulds, and cook in a bain-marie in a medium oven for about 30 minutes. Serve on salad leaves with a lemon and parsley garnish.

Fishy lemons

4 large lemons
6 oz/175 g fresh filleted sardines
1 tbsp dill, chopped
3 oz/75 g margarine
French mustard
1 egg-white
4 bay-leaves, fresh if possible, or another suitable, stiff fresh herb

Grill the sardines for 5 minutes. Leave to cool. In the meantime, cut the tops off the lemons and remove all the pulp with a spoon. Reserve it and all the juice. Mash the sardines with the chopped dill, margarine, mustard and black pepper to season. Then stir in the lemon with stiffly beaten egg-white. Check the seasoning, adjusting the mustard and pepper if necessary. Stuff the lemons with this mixture. Chill. Serve in attractive egg-cups, with dill scattered on top, and a bay-leaf stuck jauntily in the peak of the mixture.

A nest of quail's eggs

curly endive
4 oz/100 g French beans
12 quail's eggs
SALAD DRESSING
3 tbsp olive oil
1 tbsp white-wine vinegar
pepper
a pinch of mustard and sugar
CHICKEN LIVER PÂTÉ
4 oz/100 g chicken liver
1 tsp margarine
1 shallot
1 tbsp brandy
pepper
thyme
black olives and chives for garnish

Prepare the endive and arrange on a large circular plate. Steam the French beans for 5 minutes, cool, and arrange on the endive in a random, bird's-nest style. Make the pâté in advance by heating through the shallot, and then the liver, in the warm margarine for about 5 minutes. Add the brandy, pepper and fresh thyme, and sizzle for 2 minutes. Blend when still warm and leave to set.

Cut into pieces and arrange on the salad nest. Boil the quail's eggs for $1\frac{1}{2}$ minutes, arrange on the nest, pour over the dressing, and serve garnished with chives, and black olive flowers (see page 28). *Photograph on page 158.*

The prawns of love

8 giant prawns
2 oranges
1 lemon
1 lime
1 small tin of red pimentos
1 lb/450 g fresh, ripe tomatoes
1 tbsp fresh dill, if available
1 small red onion
black pepper
radicchio is optional

Marinade the prawns in the juice of 1 orange for about 2 hours. Slice the onion into fine rings, chop about a quarter of these finely and cover with lemon juice. Make a tomato pulp and pass it through a fine sieve. Do the same with the pimento and mix both together. Add the pepper and chopped dill, plus the orange and lemon juice from the marinade. Slice the second orange finely. Using 2 prawns, make a heart shape on each of the 4 white plates, add an orange slice, spoon over the sauce and decorate with onion, dill and a twist of lime. Serve with wholemeal bread. The prawns and sauce can be served on a bed of radicchio, maintaining the heart shape, if preferred. *Photograph opposite.*

Fennel with lemon

1 bulb of fennel
1 lemon
4 tbsp *fromage blanc*, the soft, more liquid type
1 tbsp parsley, chopped
pepper

Slice the fennel thinly and blanch in boiling water. Grate the lemon peel and blanch, and slice the lemon flesh. Mix both with the pepper, parsley and *fromage blanc*, and then toss with the fennel. Chill slightly before serving, garnished with lemon twists (see page 30) and parsley.

Page 155
The prawns of love. Black currant cheesecake

MAIN COURSES

Wild duck in Marsala

This recipe can be adapted for cultivated duck breasts, or for poussins.
But the sweet richness of the sauce is at its best with the stronger taste of
wild duck, like mallard.

2 mallards
2 tbsp oil
2 lemons, 1 for cooking and 1 for garnish
1½ tsp chopped lemon thyme (or common thyme),
   and extra for garnish
4 fl oz/100 ml Marsala
4 fl oz/100 ml chicken or game stock
1 onion, chopped
1 clove garlic, chopped
2 stalks celery, chopped
2 oz/50 g button mushrooms, chopped
pepper

Soften the onion, garlic, and then the celery in the oil. Push to one side
and brown the 2 ducks. Cut the lemon in half, extract the juice and keep
for later. Put a half-lemon shell into each bird with a little of the thyme,
and place the vegetables and birds into a casserole. Add the stock,
thyme and pepper, and cook in a medium oven for about an hour. In the
meantime, soak the mushrooms in the Marsala. When the birds are
cooked, remove from the casserole and keep them warm on a serving
dish. Remove the fat from the juices in the casserole, add the mushrooms and Marsala, and reduce on top of the stove until the sauce is the
right consistency. Add the lemon juice to it to sharpen the flavour,
check for seasoning, and serve with the ducks and a choice of crisp
vegetables. Garnish with fresh thyme and lemon.

Partridge with orange sauce

If the partridge are small, you may need 4 for 4 people, but if you have
eaten a substantial first course, you can get away with half a bird each.

1 onion, chopped
1 clove garlic, chopped

156

2 oz/50 g margarine

pepper

1 cup of stock, plus fat-free juices from the roasted birds

1 glass brandy

2 oranges, 1 sliced and 1 used for juice and finely cut peel

2 tbsp chopped chives, half to use in the sauce and half for garnish

Roast the partridges in the normal way. Just before they are ready, soften the chopped onion and garlic in the margarine. Add the stock and cooking brandy and boil until reduced by half. Add the juice of the orange, plus the finely chopped peel, which has been blanched and drained, pepper and chives. Reduce until a good consistency. Place the partridges on a large serving plate, pour the sauce over their tops, garnish with 1 orange slice per person and chives. Serve with new potatoes in their skins and a green vegetable, like broccoli, and carrots, sprinkled with chives, to match the colour of the oranges.

Roast wild duck with Seville sauce

This sharp, tangy sauce is perfect with wild duck, preferably roasted well. Wild duck is much lower in fat than farmed ducks, but lean ducks breasts can also be used, grilled till still pink in the centre, with this sauce.

1 tbsp margarine

1 tbsp flour

1 glass white wine

$\frac{1}{4}$ pt/150 ml stock made from duck giblets

3 Seville oranges

pepper

sugar to taste

Heat the margarine till pale brown. Add the flour and make a roux. Add the wine and stock gradually and then simmer until you have a good consistency. Remove the orange peel thinly. Cut into matchstick-size pieces and boil for 5 minutes, then drain. Squeeze out the orange juice, and add to the sauce with the pepper and sugar. Put in the peel to heat through and serve with the duck, and a fresh salad of perhaps watercress mixed with chicory, and even orange segments.

Page 158
A nest of quail's eggs

Pheasant with orange and cranberry sauce

When I see cranberries on sale, I usually think how sad it is that these inviting, juicy red spheres are so often only tasted with the Christmas turkey. Now that it is easier to find them beyond that final week in December, it is worth trying them in other recipes. This one uses cranberries with pheasant, plus another appealing part of a good greengrocer's display – kumquats. These miniature oranges look beautiful on any fresh-fruit display. They are delicious to eat whole, with their unusual, tangy taste, but they can also improve an orange sauce, and make exquisite garnishes.

2 pheasants
1 orange, plus orange slices for garnish
6 oz/175 g cranberries
4 kumquats, 2 for the sauce, 2 for garnish
3 tbsp orange liqueur, brandy or vodka
parsley and thyme, for cooking and garnish
pepper

Squeeze the orange juice, and put to one side. Place a squeezed out orange half in each pheasant, plus the herbs. Pepper the pheasants, put in roasting bags or foil, and cook in a hot oven for about 45 minutes, removing the bags or foil for the last 15 minutes.

In the meantime, simmer the cranberries in the orange juice for 4–5 minutes. Purée half the cranberries, leaving the rest whole. Take the pheasant juices, remove the fat, heat with the cranberries, sliced kumquats and alcohol until a good consistency. Serve the sauce with the pheasants, garnished with fruit and herbs.

Page 159
Roast wild duck with Seville sauce

Normandy pheasant

2 pheasants
1 oz/25 g margarine
1 onion, chopped
1 clove garlic, chopped
1 glass Calvados
1 cup stock
mixed herbs, preferably lemon thyme and bay-leaf
about 3 tbsp *fromage blanc*
4 sharp-tasting eating apples
pepper

Brown the pheasants in the margarine, then soften the chopped onion and garlic. Flame with Calvados, add the stock, sliced apples, pepper and herbs. Bring it to the boil, cover and simmer for 1 hour. Take out the pheasants, carve and arrange on a dish. Remove the herbs, and then purée the contents of the casserole. Reduce to thicken if necessary, add the *fromage blanc*, check the seasoning and serve with a celery dish and potatoes. Julienne of potato and celery, cooked over heat for several minutes, is ideal.

Grouse in red wine

2 grouse
1 oz/25 g margarine
pepper
2 lean rashers bacon
1 onion
1 clove garlic
1 cup good stock
1 glass red wine
mixed herbs
3 tbsp red currant jelly
2 oz/50 g mushrooms
few black olives

Heat the margarine and brown the grouse well. Soften the onion and bacon, and season. Add the herbs, garlic, olives, stock and wine. Add all this to the grouse in a casserole and cook in a medium oven for 1 hour. Take out, put the grouse on a dish, reduce the sauce, add the sliced mushrooms, simmer for 2 minutes, thicken with red currant jelly, check the seasoning and when the sauce is the right consistency, pour over the grouse to serve. Leeks go well with this recipe.

Jugged hare

This is a dinner party special, which uses a marinade to make the hare less rich and less dry.

1 hare, jointed	pinch of mace
2 tbsp oil	1 bay-leaf
4 glasses wine vinegar	pepper
2 onions	1 lemon
2 carrots	pinch powdered cloves
4 oz/100 g mushrooms	2 tbsp red currant jelly
2 sticks celery	port
2 cloves garlic	parsley, chopped

Marinade the hare in the wine vinegar for 24 hours. Drain, dry and brown in the oil. Put in a casserole, and then cook the vegetables in the oil. Add to the hare with the stock, mace, cloves, herb, garlic, lemon juice and a strip of the rind. Cook the casserole in a moderate oven for 2 hours, then reduce the temperature to low and cook for another 1–2 hours. Reduce the liquid, add the port and red currant jelly. Serve the hare with the sauce poured over and garnished with fresh parsley. Serve with potatoes in their skins, crisp green vegetables – and some extra red currant jelly (home-made if possible).

Wild rabbit with a port and damson sauce

This recipe is also excellent with wild duck instead of rabbit.

1 rabbit, jointed	1 glass port
$\frac{1}{2}$ lb/225 g damsons	pepper
1 onion	$\frac{1}{2}$ tbsp flour
1 clove garlic	1 tbsp oil
1 tbsp hyssop, chopped	pinch of mace

*Page 163
Jugged hare*

Cover the rabbit joints in seasoned flour, and brown in the oil. Soften the chopped onion and garlic in a casserole, put the rabbit on top with the herb, mace, and stoned damsons. Finally, add the port and cook in a medium oven for $1\frac{1}{2}$ to 2 hours. Reduce the juices just before serving, if necessary. Garnish with a few whole cooked damsons or poached damsons, and sprigs of hyssop.

Mustard rabbit

I also make this rabbit dish with my orange mustard (see page 173) and use the juice of an orange in the sauce. It is excellent with this refreshing, fruity change of ingredients.

1 good rabbit cut into pieces
2 tbsp flour
black pepper
3 tbsp oil
1 onion, finely chopped
1 clove garlic, finely chopped
hyssop, or mixed herbs if it is not available
1 glass white wine
1 cup chicken stock
2 tsp French mustard
1 tsp English mustard
4 oz/100 g plain low-fat yoghurt

Roll the rabbit in the flour. Season and brown in oil. Add the onion, garlic, herbs, wine and stock, and simmer until tender. Take out the rabbit, add the mustards and yoghurt to pan. Simmer the sauce until the right consistency. Add the rabbit to heat through and serve, garnished with fresh herbs.

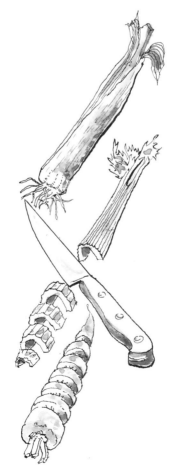

Turkey with ginger sauce

12 lb/5.5 kg turkey. Roast this as normal, but on a bed of chopped vegetables. Use:
2 carrots
4 leeks
4 celery stalks
thyme
parsley
bay-leaf
SAUCE
1 onion, chopped finely
1 clove garlic, chopped
1 inch/2.5 cm piece of fresh ginger, grated
1 glass ginger wine
1 tbsp oil
6 fl oz/175 ml stock made from turkey giblets
10 oz/275 g chestnuts

Shell the chestnuts and cook them till tender in the stock. Remove half, and liquidize the rest. Soften the onion, garlic and then the ginger in the oil. Add the purée of chestnuts in turkey stock and simmer for several minutes. Add some of the juices from the cooked turkey and the ginger wine, and reduce this sauce until it is the ideal consistency. Serve the turkey garnished with whole chestnuts, and the ginger sauce. The bed of vegetables, used when cooking the turkey, makes a tasty soup.

Pork with quince and honey

During the dull winter months, friends can be invited round for meals to remind them of recent, sunny holidays abroad. If Greece was their destination, try the following Greek feast: traditional egg and lemon soup; followed by hummus; taramasalata; yoghurt with cucumber; and perhaps a Greek salad too, made with Feta cheese, black olives, tomatoes and cucumber. Try pork with quince as a main course, followed by Greek pastries, made with filo pastry, nuts and honey.

2 lb/900 g pork fillet, cubed
2 tbsp oil
2 onions, chopped
2 cloves garlic, crushed
2 glasses red wine
strip of orange peel
pinch of powdered cinnamon
$\frac{1}{2}$ pt/300 ml stock
1 lb/450 g quince, peeled, cored and sliced
2 tbsp honey
pepper
chopped coriander leaves for garnish

Soften the onions and garlic in the hot oil, push to one side and brown the meat. Put in the cinnamon, orange peel, wine and stock. Simmer covered for 1 hour. Then add the quince, pepper and honey, and cook gently for another hour, until the quince are tender. Taste for seasoning. If the quince have made it too sharp, add a little more honey. Serve scattered with chopped coriander.

PUDDINGS

DRIED FRUIT

Dried fruits, especially prunes, have a dull image, and I find that if I serve them straight, with a choice of other desserts, they will inevitably be left. But their taste can be excellent, and when I serve them disguised, they always get plenty of praise. I love them so much, and they are useful and healthy to serve in winter when fresh local fruit has been forgotten. Therefore, I make a lot of effort to find special ways of serving mixed dried fruits, prunes, and especially apricots. I find that many dried fruits contain enough sugar naturally, so I do not include any in my recipes. If necessary, it can always be added later. Cooking times given are usually too long, leaving you with a soggy unappealing mess. Just soaking the fruit can often be enough, but it is difficult to be precise because the age of dried fruit varies. So test after soaking, and only cook any fruit which still seems tough. I think a little chewiness is part of the appeal.

Compote of brandied fruits

1 lb/450 g mixed dried fruit
1 lemon
4 tbsp brandy
2 oz/50 g toasted flaked almonds
8 oz/225 g brandy snaps
yoghurt snow (see page 65) flavoured with brandy

Soak the fruit overnight in cold water. If any need cooking, simmer briefly with a little lemon rind added to the juices. If the fruit needs extra sugar, add it just before cooking. Then add the brandy and lemon juice, and leave for an hour or two, for the fruit to absorb the flavour.

Chop up half the fruit, including all the prunes, leaving the most attractive fruits whole. Stuff the brandy snaps with the chopped fruit, arrange them with the whole fruits attractively on a plate. Warm through in the oven very briefly, and serve sprinkled with almonds. Offer brandy yoghurt snow in a separate bowl.

Page 167
Compote of brandied fruits

Stuffed apricots

8 oz/225 g dried apricots
a pinch of cinnamon
1 glass dry white wine
2 oz/50 g toasted almonds
6 oz/175 g thick *fromage blanc*

Soak the apricots overnight. Drain, and simmer with the wine and cinnamon for about 10 minutes. Leave to cool in the wine juices. Open up each apricot and fill with a little *fromage blanc*, and arrange attractively on a serving dish with a sauce. Scatter the toasted nuts on top.

Hedgehog fruit soufflé

8 oz/225 g mixed dried fruit
4 oz/100 g dry white wine
4 egg-whites
2 oz/50 g split almonds
thick, plain yoghurt

Wash the fruit well and then leave to soak in water overnight. If the fruit is soft, no cooking is required; if not, simmer for 5 minutes or so. Drain, and leave to cool. Then soak the fruit a little longer in the wine. Then chop very finely, whisk the egg-whites until stiff, and fold into the fruit and wine mixture. Put the mixture in an oval dish, spike with split almonds and bake for 20 minutes. Serve immediately with thick, plain yoghurt.

Mango and lime ice-cream

2 ripe mangos
juice of 2 limes
8 oz/225 g plain thick yoghurt
2 tbsp honey
2 tbsp tequila

Cut the mangos in half and scrape out the flesh. Purée. Mix with the other ingredients, and make into ice-cream in the normal way. Serve with slices of mango, and mint garnish.

Passion-fruit and banana ice-cream

This can be served on a coulis of passion-fruit and Kirsch, and garnished with banana and mint.

4 passion-fruit
2 bananas
8 oz/225 g plain thick yoghurt
2 tbsp honey

Halve the passion-fruits and scoop out the flesh. Make a purée with this and the bananas. Stir in the honey and yoghurt, and make the ice-cream in the normal way, described on page 64.

Sharp and sweet winter salad

1 large pineapple
juice of 1 lemon
4 oz/100 g dried apricots
4 oz/100 g fresh dates
¼ pt/150 ml dry white wine
mint for garnish

Soak the apricots in dry white wine overnight. If they are not soft enough, simmer in the wine for a few minutes, then leave to cool. Cut off the top of the pineapple and keep as an attractive lid for the final dessert. Scoop out the pineapple flesh, cut into bite-size pieces and put in a bowl with the cool apricots in their wine sauce, lemon juice, and the dates. Toss them together, then pile back into the pineapple, and serve with the pineapple top back in place, garnished with mint.

HOW TO HAVE YOUR CHRISTMAS AND EAT IT

Christmas is an exhausting time, which can be ruined by overwork in the kitchen, unless you find ways of taking short cuts. It is a time for families and friends, a holiday time, and I think the most special few days of the year. So if it is going to be a success, I belive it has to be regarded as a sort of exam where you are allowed to cheat. I have not always taken this attitude. In the past I used to produce complicated food, which demanded last-minute attention, as a result I used to get very little attention from my family and friends.

Now I ask our guests to share by bringing contributions. Perhaps the most successful was when a Swiss au pair wanted to stay in England for Christmas, rather than going home. She made chocolates, Swiss cakes and biscuits and on Christmas morning itelf, baked a stunning plaited loaf. In turn she learned about plum pudding and traditional stuffings for turkey. Now, apparently, her Christmas dinners are 'en style Anglais'.

I stock up my freezer with fish pâtés, terrines, sorbets and home-made ice-creams for weeks beforehand. I have home-made relishes and preserves ready to eat with the inevitable cold meats, and I buy plenty of good pasta and salad produce to make quick, light meals.

Christmas Day itself is very traditional with a locally reared, large turkey if there are more than six of us, and a goose for a quieter day. On Boxing Day I normally roast a lean whole gammon with orange, mace, brown sugar and cider, and serve it with home-made Cumberland sauce. Pudding ideas include mixed dried fruit inside brandy snaps, or in filo pastry, shaped like Christmas crackers. Or when the food has been too rich, fresh-fruit salad is better, using exotic fruits like lychees, mango and papaya.

Goose is perhaps the favourite in our household. The first year of my marriage somebody gave us one because we were short of money. They also gave us an old copper coal-scuttle, so we carried the goose home in that. Regrettably, the old gas oven in our shabby flat couldn't cope, and we ate the bird a day later than we had planned. Nowadays, I usually stuff it with a mixture dominated by the taste of pickled walnuts. We have a tree in the garden and pickle our own fleshy fruit in July, before the nuts have formed, using a recipe from Mrs Beaton's old book. This is my recipe for using those pickled walnuts at Christmas time.

Page 171
Food for presents

Goose stuffing

6 pickled walnuts, cut into quarters
3 tbsp fresh sage, chopped
2½ cups breadcrumbs
2 onions, chopped
1 oz/25 g margarine
2 sharp apples
grated rind and juice of 1 lemon
pepper
stock from giblets

Soften the onions in the margarine. Add the sage and then mix in all the other ingredients.

Turkey stuffing

I like to make a very fruity stuffing for the turkey. This is moist, and mixes well with cranberry sauce and port, brussel sprouts with chestnuts, and all the other traditional extras.

5 oz/150 g dried apricots, soaked overnight and cut into 6 pieces
1 small head celery, chopped, keeping the inner part to eat with cheese
4 oz/100 g walnuts, chopped
1 oz/25 g margarine
1 large onion
2 cups breadcrumbs
1 tbsp parsley
1 tbsp thyme
pepper

Soften the onions in the margarine. Add the celery for 3 minutes, and then mix with the other ingredients.

FOOD FOR PRESENTS

Food makes a perfect present for friends. A consumable gift is appreciated by those lucky people who seem to have everything. It becomes a relief and a real pleasure to receive very special, far-from-everyday food. And for poorer friends who are forced to eat unexciting food, an exotic pâté or a jar of wonderful preserves is particularly welcome. Pâtés of all kinds; home-made mustards, like the simple orange mustard I make as presents every Christmas; strings of dried ceps; large bunches of dried herbs tied in festive red ribbon; and preserves, like my special quince or orange (see page 140) and spiced crab-apples (see page 141), are ideal.

Kipper and coriander pâté

When I am making fish and game pâtés to store in the freezer for Christmas, I often make smaller ones to give to friends who do not enjoy cooking. I am always looking for pretty containers to use for these presents. This recipe is quick to make, and refreshing at Christmas or any time of the year.

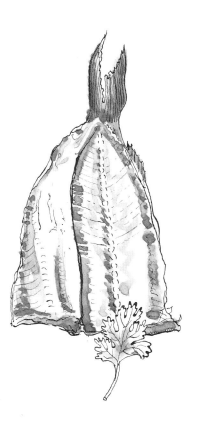

4 oz/100 g kipper fillets, cooked in the normal way
juice of $\frac{1}{2}$ lemon
3 oz/75 g soft margarine
1 tbsp coriander, chopped
1 tsp tomato purée
pepper
pinch of mace

Purée all the ingredients. Pack into a pretty pot and decorate with coriander.

Orange mustard

Herb mustards and oils can be made in the summer when the herb garden is harvested, using the best olive oil and French mustard. Pack them in pretty jars. Or try this unusual mustard.

For each juicy orange you will need 3 tablespoons of good French mustard. Peel the orange and blend the flesh with the mustard. Put it in a pot and when it has set a little, garnish with a very thin orange slice. This is good with lean ham, or for cooking with pork fillet.

Clementines in brandy

These make a perfect present for someone who really deserves a big 'thank-you'. These festive, small fruit, which are a cross between tangerines and bitter oranges, look exotic in smart, clear-glass storage jars.

1 lb/450 g of the smallest clementines you can find
cheap brandy
syrup made from 1 pt/600 ml water and 8 oz/225 g sugar
vanilla pods

Prick the fruit all over with a sharp fork or knife, and simmer in the syrup mixture for an hour. Strain and put into pretty glass jars. Pour in the brandy to half-way up the fruit and then top up with the syrup. Put a vanilla pod in each jar. They taste at their best after a month or more. They are very rich, and should only be eaten one at a time, as a dessert after a special meal.

Page 175
Aphrodisiacs

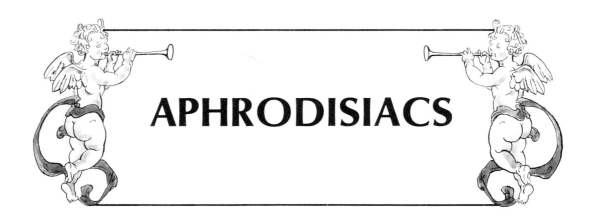

APHRODISIACS

When you first looked at *The Food of Love*, some of you may have believed that it was a book about aphrodisiacs, or 'foods which stimulate sexual desire'. You will now know that my book is really only about the 'aphrodisiac' available to us all, which is the ability and urge to rustle up that little extra something to make a meal memorable and romantic.

However, there are centuries of folklore, and the beginnings of some serious scientific studies, which back up the claims that certain foods can encourage romance. So, in the true spirit of adventure, I include recipes here, using ingredients which *might* just be aphrodisiacs.

I will start with those centuries of folklore. The definition: 'Aphrodisiacks, Things that excite Lust or Venery' appeared in an early dictionary, the *Glossographia Anglicana Nova* of 1719. But the name comes from Aphrodite, the Greek Goddess of Love, who is said to have risen naked from the sea on a scallop shell, near Paphos, in Cyprus. That is one reason why scallops are on the long list of foods with aphrodisiac reputations.

Lobster, mussels, and oysters are also considered to be aphrodisiacs because of the 'fish' association with Aphrodite. Oysters are perhaps the most famous of all romantic foods, and were used by many famous lovers. Casanova was said to eat fifty of them every day for breakfast. British oysters were highly praised by the Romans and were once a commonly available and very cheap food, classed as only fit for the poor. How things have changed!

They are still relatively cheap in France, and very cheap in the United States where I sat in a jazz club in New Orleans and washed raw oysters down with champagne – and in Florida where at happy hour I could get four for a dollar. Let's hope the attempts to breed the Pacific oyster in British waters will bring prices down – even if connoisseurs say the quality is not as good as that of the traditional oyster.

There may even be something in the claims that oysters encourage romance. These shellfish are a rich source of zinc, and scientists have discovered that women can become infertile if the level of zinc in their bodies becomes too low. Zinc is also lost in ejaculation.

At the other end of the price scale, the humble potato is also said to have aphrodisiac qualities. When potatoes were first introduced to Europe in the sixteenth century, they were only popular at first as aphrodisiacs, selling for as much as £250 per pound. And remember, at that time, it would take twenty years to earn that sum.

Peaches are said to be yet another aphrodisiac, with the Arabs and Chinese believing the downy cleft of the peach symbolic of the female reproductive organs. Avocado pears may have a more scientific basis for their reputation. They contain a lot of Vitamin E, which some researchers believe is essential to prevent sterility and impotence.

Black currants are yet another fruit with supposed aphrodisiac qualities. I cannot vouch for that, but I do know that I love them, and use them a great deal in savoury as well as dessert recipes. I also use a lot of the blackcurrant liqueur, *Crème de Cassis*, in my recipes. The drink Kir, a dash of *Cassis* in dry white wine, is apparently named after a past Mayor of Dijon, Canon Felix Kir, who lived to be 92, due it is said by some, to his enthusiasm for *Cassis*. I use both blackcurrants and the liqueur in many recipes, like with kidneys (see page 86), and in a delicious cheesecake (see page 97).

Other foods which are rumoured to be aphrodisiacs include asparagus, blackberries, broccoli, leeks, parsnips, spinach and tomatoes. I do not personally believe a word of it, but the stories are good fun, and all these foods are delicious anyway. If I did believe that, say oysters, were a great stimulant, I think it would put me off serving them to any man. It would seem to obvious a statement, just like wearing an unsubtle see-through blouse.

Lobster thermidor

Lobster is now so expensive that it rarely makes an appearance in my life. But when it does, it always seems to be on an exciting and memorable occasion.

My first taste was on one of our many family holidays on the North-East coast near Sunderland. My older brother, who was eleven, achieved his ambition by catching one on a hook. Years later I cooked lobster for the first time when a local fisherman in Gozo, near Malta, hauled one for me from the sea. Since then I have eaten lobster, complete with a garish lobster bib around my neck, in Cape Cod. I have enjoyed it plain and simple in County Kerry, Dublin, Florida and St Lucia: always on very special occasions, which is how it must be with such an extravagant dish. This is how I cooked lobster recently for a friend who provided the shellfish on condition that I did the cooking.

2 lobsters
1 shallot, chopped
several crushed peppercorns
1 tbsp wine vinegar
1 glass dry white wine
1 oz/25 g margarine
$\frac{3}{4}$ pt/450 ml hot milk
2 tbsp flour
4 tbsp *fromage frais*
French mustard to taste
pepper
2 oz/50 g Gruyère, grated
2 tbsp breadcrumbs
2 lemons
tarragon (optional)

Boil the lobsters in the normal way. Then split them in half, clean, remove the inedible parts, chop the flesh and add the meat from the claws to it. Boil the wine, vinegar, peppercorns and shallot mixture until reduced by half. Add the margarine, stir in the flour when melted, and then add the hot milk. Simmer until smooth, sieve, and then flavour with the mustard and pepper. Add the *fromage frais* gently until well mixed. Pour this sauce on to the lobster halves, add the cheese and breadcrumbs and brown under the grill. Serve with lemon. Tarragon can be used to flavour the sauce, and as a garnish, if liked.

Scallops with golden sauce

The legend of the birth of Aphrodite is still alive in Cyprus. Thousands of people every year go down to the beach near Paphos where she is said to have appeared out of the sea so many years ago. I have to admit that, although I have been there three or four times, I have yet to see the image of this golden goddess rise up from the waves. This recipe has amatory connections because the scallop was first thought of as the womb that enclosed Aphrodite. Later it was to become her raft.

16 scallops
⅓ pt/200 ml dry white wine
pinch mace
pinch of powdered cloves
grated rind and juice of 1 Seville orange
chopped tarragon (or parsley) and herb to garnish

Simmer the wine and spices for 5 minutes. Check for flavour, then add the scallops and simmer for another 5 minutes. Remove the scallops, slice and keep warm. Add the orange to the sauce, and reduce it. Add the herbs and check the flavour. Add a little sugar if this seems necessary. Serve on a bed of salad leaves, or on rice if preferred.

Caviare with oysters

Both ingredients are expensive, but at least this luxurious first course only requires small quantities. Always serve caviare simply, in a dish packed with ice, plus lemon and wholemeal or dark rye bread. For each portion, place 1 tablespoon of caviare on a dish, make a hollow in the centre, and put a fresh oyster in it. Use a little lemon juice, and even less black pepper.

Truffles

Truffles are ridiculously expensive because they are extremely rare. So rare, that animals have to be found to locate them by smell. Attempts have been made to cultivate these edible fungi in quantity, using tissue culture. But the experts say they do not taste the same, so they continue to cost the earth, at over £100 per pound for the real thing.

It is claimed that in the past many people, including Rabelais and the Marquis de Sade, ate them for their aphrodisiac qualities, although today's enthusiasts are more interested in their taste. I am lucky enough to have a truffle expert as a friend, and have tasted fresh, white truffles, grated over his own delicious risottos. Fresh truffles do make the tinned versions seem tame. I am not a regular truffle user, but one recipe I have cooked at home is pheasant breasts with truffles.

INDEX